LIVING TRUE TO YOU

Inspirational Stories of Self-Doubt,
Self-Discovery and Embracing Your Destiny

COMPILED BY CATHERINE CHAN-KWA

Copyright © 2022 to Catherine Chan-Kwa

ALL RIGHTS RESERVED. No part of this book may be reproduced, stored in, or introduced into a retrieval system, or transmitted, in any form, or by any means, including photocopying, recording or other electronic or mechanical methods or reproduced in any other manner whatsoever without written permission by the publisher, except in the case of brief quotations within critical articles or reviews and certain other noncommercial uses permitted by copyright law.

PUBLISHED BY: Your Shift Matters Publishing, a division of Dana Zarcone International, LLC

DISCLAIMER AND/OR LEGAL NOTICES

While all attempts have been made to verify information provided in this book and its ancillary materials, neither the authors or publisher assumes any responsibility for errors, inaccuracies or omissions in the information provided and is not responsible for any financial loss by customer in any manner. Any slights of people or organisations are unintentional. If advice concerning legal, financial, accounting, or related matters is needed, the services of a qualified professional should be sought. This book is for inspirational purposes only. The views expressed in this book are based on the author's own personal experience or the outcomes with clients that they may have personally witnessed.

The compiler, publisher and authors do not assume any responsibility or liability whatsoever on the behalf of the purchaser or reader of these materials. The authors and publisher shall in no way, under any circumstances, be held liable to any party (or third party) for any direct, indirect, punitive, special, incidental or other consequential damages arising directly or indirectly from the content in this book and any use of books, materials and or seminar trainings, which is provided "as is," and without warranties.

Publisher: Your Shift Matters Publishing, a Division of Dana Zarcone International, LLC

Book Cover and Formatting by Let's Get Booked
www.letsgetbooked.com

ISBN: 978-1-7378234-1-4

Gratitude

I want to start by showing my appreciation for all the authors of this book who, like myself, have a passion for serving others and making the world a better place. I feel blessed, honoured and grateful to have you on this journey with me.

We've come together to share our stories in hopes that it will touch the lives of others and inspire them to live all-in and full-out. To inspire them to shift from simply surviving to totally thriving in all aspects of their lives. I know some, if not all of you, are taking a big risk. Maybe you're revealing yourself in a way that's never been done before, or you're telling a story that's never been told before. Either way, I know that, by sharing your stories, you will touch many hearts and ignite many spirits. Thank you! I hope this journey has been as amazing for you as it has been for me!

The past few years have been full of some serious ups and downs. Some of which I'm sure I'll tell you about someday soon. For now, suffice it to say I wouldn't be where I am today without so many beautiful people in my life. People who support me, love me and even give me a swift, well-needed kick in the keister at times. I'm grateful for all that they do!

I'm especially grateful to the friends, mentors and coaches I've worked with over the years. You have been instrumental in showing me all the amazing ways I can own my brilliance, help people own theirs and make the world a better place.

Thank you for pushing me and encouraging me to never give up – even though there were times when I wanted to!

In addition, the one person that had a significant influence in my life is my mother. She always believed in me, even when I didn't believe in myself. Today, she's still my cheerleader.

Thanks, Lai Ngor Mak. Without you I would not be where I am today.

I want to thank my publisher, Dana Zarcone, for saying "YES" to this anthology! I had a vision and knew I had chosen the right person to teach me the ropes and guide me. It's an honour to call you my friend, and I love you! Thank you for your guidance, leadership, and ongoing support of my writing and publishing!

Finally, I am so grateful for Kelvin Kwa, my husband and soul mate, his never-ending love and my number one fan. Alex Kwa, my son, is my inspiration and my reason for everything. Thank you all very much for your love and support. To my sisters, I will say that I hope I'm able to inspire you, just as my mom inspired me, to follow your dreams and never give up! Remember to be confident and always… live true to you!

With love,

Catherine Chan-Kwa

Table of Contents

Introduction 1

Chapter 1:
Living True to You by Catherine Chan-Kwa 4

Chapter 2:
My Fry Pan Moment by Evie Csapo 16

Chapter 3:
The Universe Burned My Lifeboats by Linda Ho 33

Chapter 4:
The Magic of Your Heart by Lisa Jowett 40

Chapter 5:
The Silent Whisper of the 'Good Mother' by Linh Le 51

Chapter 6:
Silver Linings by Carmen Louise 65

Chapter 7:
Forgiveness Snapshot by Ana O'Brien 75

Chapter 8:
Becoming a Courageous Woman by Kate Southall 86

Chapter 9:
The Most Precious Commodity by Grace Wee 96

Conclusion 107

INTRODUCTION

A myriad of reasons and motivations may have brought you here to our book, *Living True to You*. Perhaps you like the look of the cover, perhaps the title is intriguing, the spine is just the right thickness for some light afternoon reading or…maybe you're looking for something deeper, more meaningful.

Perhaps you are seeking some insight, guidance or relief for your particular situation. You may find the answers you seek within these pages; however, this book does not purport to be the source of existential truth.

In my youth, a wise mentor once told me that every belief, argument, opinion and perspective thought to be absolute could often be undermined by doubt and ambiguity. For every position we hold, there is an equally valid opposing point of view, often more than one. Hence, there is only one type of truth in all the universe that is unassailable.

The personal story…

An individual's true account of events, what they experienced, what they did and how it made them feel. Every aspect is unique to the storyteller, thus it cannot be challenged.

In this book, nine women share their personal stories in hopes of inspiring you. They have lived through their share of triumphs and tragedies, highs and lows. They are just like you and me but what sets them apart is that one day, they found the courage to ask themselves the hard questions.

Is this all there is?

Is this all I deserve?

Am I satisfied with what my life has become?

Is there more out there for me?

How do I get there?

These women have chosen to break through the limiting beliefs that have been indoctrinated into their psyche, reach out and explore their limitless potential. They have chosen to live as the best versions of themselves, to live true to the amazing, powerful and deserving individuals that they now know themselves to be.

These are their stories. The undisputed truths you find inside are their gift to you.

Welcome to Living True to You!

CATHERINE CHAN-KWA

Catherine Chan-Kwa is a visionary fuelled by her desire to support professional women and empower them to reach their full spiritual and personal potential in their careers, business, marriage and motherhood.

A practising mental health clinician for over 20 years, Catherine applies her holistic philosophy of healing and enrichment to body, soul and spirit, with integrative therapies helping women live true to themselves.

As a business and life coach, she loves seeing professional women radiant within themselves, reign over their business and career with creativity while significantly contributing to the world.

Catherine is happily married and a proud mother of one after a long infertility journey. She enjoys pursuing freedom, fun and dreams.

Contact Catherine: https://m.me/cathkwa
FB: https://www.facebook.com/cathkwa
Website: https://www.catherinechankwacoaching.com/

Chapter 1

Living True to You

By Catherine Chan-Kwa

I was born Hoi-Yan Chan in Hong Kong Island in January 1973. Was it a dark and stormy night? No. Were there signs and portents in the skies above the hospital? Maybe. But let me qualify that.

It was probably just some people with poor impulse control setting off Chinese New Year fireworks three days early. January's a little cold in Hong Kong. Despite the northern hemisphere's seasonal chill, nobody on the island would pass up the chance to celebrate, to be festive, and heap upon each other the wishes and blessings of auspicious fortune.

So, if I was born into a family, society and culture which was heavily superstitious (which I was), then by that measure, I began my life under innocuous circumstances.

Now that we've established that I am not the devil's spawn, what's with all the fucking rejection?

My mother gave me my English name: Catherine. She got to name me after she won a bet with my father. She wanted a girl, and my father wanted a boy. He wanted a son to be the first born and carry the family name.

So, I grew up with an unconscious desire for my father's approval that, in turn, projected my inner insecurities onto others...

Daddy issues.

Ah, rejection. I wouldn't call you my old friend, but as the days progressed, you became my constant companion.

Rejection manifested itself in so many ways:

Bullied in kindergarten...

Primary school...

High school...

It had a significant impact on my life. The first thing I do when I arrive at a party is 'read the room'. Actually, scratch that. I scan and analyse every living soul within my sight -- even babies and pets. Yeah, no exceptions.

Why? Because nothing motivates my pathological need to catalogue every conceivable threat to my self-esteem than fear. The fear of rejection.

I began to wonder if I was the one projecting a certain perception of myself, that others were simply reacting to an image I was broadcasting at them.

Was this my fault?!

That's when I knew I'd hit rock bottom. When I started to blame myself for the injustices perpetrated on me. That morsel of insight hit me early on, but I didn't have the motivation to do anything about it. I told myself that it was just a phase and that I would grow out of it.

Turning 'Sweet Sixteen' comes with many pop culture associations: Cars with fins, rock and roll, jeans, dresses, leather jackets, spring times and summers, where high school proms become fertile ground for romance... and every other cliche that comes from watching too many episodes of Happy Days. To GenY, GenZ, Baby Boomers or Millennials, the sucrose-laden imagery may look a little different, but it all serves to impart the idea that in Western Society, turning sixteen is a wondrous time, the last great coming-of-age adventure before, well, coming of age.

But, it's not all a pack of lies made to sell you fries and a Coke with that cheeseburger. The age of sixteen isn't actually a hard frontier of transition and transformation. Change happens all the time. Some of us just notice it more when we turn sixteen. For me, as it was for my father, those changes were more bitter than sweet. We both left our hometown when we were sixteen in search of a better future. Two generations...

People thought I was joking when I shared my father's story, where at age sixteen he swam across the sea from Canton to Hong Kong. This is what the hope for a better future can motivate a person to do.

Did I have that kind of hope in me? I would like to think so. But, even then, some part of me was my father's daughter sharing in his strength and determination. I wanted to be the kind of person that would not let a mere ocean stand between me and my dreams.

When I turned sixteen, my parents bought me a plane ticket to Australia to escape the undefined threat of China's takeover of Hong Kong in the 1990's. The fact that I was not required to swim the South China Sea to get to the promised land was the only break I would get for years to come.

I got off the plane, a young girl alone in a strange land full of strange people going about their daily lives in strange ways. On the bright side, since I didn't speak the language, I would not be burdened by what they really thought of me. Ignorance can be bliss if you know how to wield it. I just smiled vacuously and got on with the job of inconspicuously working my way up the ladder of life to come out on top. And because of this asymmetric philosophy, they never saw me coming.

Sometimes, the long game in an Asian culture doesn't come to fruition in a single generation. My parents worked hard and paid for my education, propelling me forward to a better life -- better than the best hopes they had for themselves when they turned sixteen.

Armed (or burdened) with the knowledge that the previous generation's hopes and dreams rested squarely on my shoulders, I buried myself in my studies. But that would just be too easy… Study hard, work hard, and your dreams will come true? *I wish!*

My language difficulties lent another dimension, making it difficult to understand and absorb the lessons from the textbooks. Book reports were an even bigger nightmare. If I was going to succeed, I would have to dig deeper, go to the source of the problem. So, I put my books down and focused on the painstaking task of learning to speak (and read) The Queen's English.

The detour paid off, and soon after I graduated high school, I was well on my way to realising my vocational goal of becoming a psychologist. I wanted to help people, to begin the healing at the most fundamental level: the mind. Unfortunately, the challenges would only get tougher from here.

Remember my old acquaintance, rejection?

Somewhere in the middle of my psychology degree, I was told in no uncertain terms by a senior lecturer whom I admired, that he found it hard to give me clients to practice on because I was twenty-four and lacked, in his words, "life experience".

I was told, "You cannot."

I don't particularly appreciate someone telling me what I'm capable of accomplishing.

I got around that closed-minded fossil by taking the hardest posting, the one nobody wanted, tackling head-on the worst-case scenario to get that "life experience" he valued so damned much: drug rehab counselling during the graveyard shift, in the middle of one of the most economically and socially challenging suburbs in Melbourne. As Frank Sinatra says, "If you can make it there, you can make it anywhere."

Emerging from that crucible, I finally registered as a psychologist in 2000. I met some like-minded colleagues along the way, and we became friends. After sharing my entrepreneurial vision of starting my own private practice, I invited them to join me, and they said, "Sure. After you're successful, then I'll join you."

Wow, that was fast. You sure you don't want to think about it for a bit?

You could say they were just being understandably cautious. But we were close. They knew my story, and what I had overcome. Some of these individuals even shared a part of the journey with me. They knew what I was capable of.

So where in the hell was all this caution coming from? Rejection. There you are.

So, I went it alone. I built my reputation from the ground up in the public sector, private sector, educational counselling, international students, and medical practices. After a while, tertiary college institutions would invite me to take charge of their counselling departments. Doctors wanted me to attend their clinics as the onsite counsellor. I was in great demand.

I worked sixty to seventy hours a week managing staff, and dealing with stakeholders and clients… I had no time for myself, my friends or my family.

In 2003, I met my soulmate, Kelvin. Here was finally a guy who believed in me, in what I could do and what I could become. It came natural to him, but of course, once we were married, it turned into the unspoken understanding between us:

Support me in everything I do.

If you can't support me, don't get in my way!

We've been married almost 20 years, and he always has my back.

Ten years ago, I reached a turning point.

But first, a little backstory…

In 2005, when we were just a couple of young newlyweds, we thought we would one day have kids. We wanted to know the joys of parenthood but decided we would enjoy each other's company first. Like many young people, we thought we had time.

Fast forward to 2009, and there we were, just the two of us! Kelvin and I had a strong relationship. Sure, we disagreed occasionally, but the marriage was going strong. There were no secrets between us!

It was time to start thinking seriously about starting a family.

We thought we would not need any medical help. *We were wrong!*

Then, 2012 rolled into 2013, and we were two years into the emotional roller coaster of in vitro fertilisation, or IVF. An understated sense of despair had set in, and we began looking for alternatives. Perhaps, we weren't meant to be biological parents. But I was not convinced. I wanted to know the joy of carrying a life to term, of childbirth, of holding a baby in my arms made from the same stardust as I was.

But Kelvin saw multiple failed IVF attempts and five resulting miscarriages take their toll on me, and he wasn't going to let the suffering continue. You see, he remembered to be grateful for what he had… Me.

But that decision to call it was balanced with his intimate knowledge of my desires, so he told the specialist that we were willing to give it one… last… try.

And such was his commitment that he literally tried anything to ensure success.

You know how men are psychologically averse to needles? Stab them, shoot them, blow them up, but something about needles affects them on a primordial level. Well, that 'anything' turned out to be Alice, a respected acupuncturist with a reputation for success, particularly in the field of reproductive sciences and IVF.

Once a week for ten weeks, Alice turned the both of us into pin cushions. Of course, Kelvin was right beside me for all of it.

In March 2013, the last egg was fertilised, and an embryo was implanted. Weeks later, still there, still growing. We made it to June and hope was rising fast, we had never come this far before.

June became August, and preparations for the new arrival were underway. Our miracle arrived in mid-December: Alexander (Kelvin named him after Lex Luthor, the only human brave enough to go up against Superman) Eugene Kwa and he's been eating us out of house and home ever since.

During those years of uncertainty, when despair set in, I would ask myself, what did I do to get myself into this situation?

The epiphany was that, in the pursuit of commercial and professional success, I stopped connecting with people. I stopped connecting with myself, with nature and with God.

The answer for me was that I needed to live an authentic life, as I welcomed my child into this world and enjoyed the moments with Kelvin. The lesson I took from that time was that I needed to constantly remind myself to be grateful for what I have and not dwell negatively on what I don't.

In times of adversity, I realise how much I needed Kelvin and how much he needed me. That can only come from a bond that transcends romance into the realms of an intimate commitment and knowledge of each other. Simply LOVE. But with all due respect to poets and dreamers, love does NOT conquer all. There was still the small matter of my constant fear of rejection. That shit just doesn't go away! In fact, the more you have, the stronger the fear whispers in your ear about all the things you have to lose.

One day, not long ago, an insidious thought came to me: What would I do if I was rejected by Kelvin? Instead of retreating in the face of this terrible thought, I got mad. And I turned all my attention to defeating this adversary.

There's an adage from Sun Tzu's, *The Art of War*. It says, "Know your enemy. Know yourself."

This is true, especially when you realise that you can be your own enemy, but in a good way.

I finally found the source of all the rejection I had felt in my life. I used to compare myself to everyone else. That usually didn't end well. Inevitably, I would focus on my shortcomings rather than my strengths. There was always someone better than me; faster, stronger, had more money… just more of everything.

The answer came to me one day while I was out for a walk. Nothing kills self-esteem like going up the Thousand Steps in the Dandenong Ranges. No matter how fleet of foot I was, someone else would always blow right by me. Sometimes those that passed were children, sometimes the elderly, and occasionally just wildlife that seemed prevalent in these parts. The place was rife with inner city fitness fanatics and wellness professionals. And let me tell you, they come in all different shapes and sizes. I had a thousand steps and a thousand ways to criticise myself.

That's when it hit me. I want, no, I need to be my own enemy. I need to compete with the only person whose opinion matters: *Mine*! And with that realisation, my old adversary, rejection, lost its sting. The fear evaporated.

From that day forward, I chose to test only myself, constantly beating my personal best. And little by little, step by step, I found myself welcoming all the challenges ahead of me.

We are living in interesting times. In Asian traditions, that's a curse. With lockdowns, pandemics, natural disasters and rumours of war, it may seem that way, but there is also light in the darkness and much hope. There is also the challenge before you to make a choice. You can choose to see the bad in the world or find the good, regardless of what's happening.

We are all so much more aware of each other now. We are united in our willingness to help each other and to look, *really look* inward to find out who we are to ourselves and each other.

My journey now is about taking a good long look at my own life and how I will get to that place where I live a life that is true to my passions, dreams and desires. I've shared pieces of my story, history, culture, and philosophies. I've shared the things I've learned and the promise of things to come.

You see it, don't you? I'm not that different from you. I took that first step - then another and another - until I could not imagine being anywhere else but here on this journey of self-discovery. Now, it's the most natural thing. It's like I finally belong.

Why not join me?

My contact details are included in this book. Call me, email me, find me and connect. I am Catherine Chan-Kwa…

and I'm right here with you!

Evie Csapo

Evie Csapo, founder of Precious Mettle Coaching, is known to many of her friends, family and students as the "Resilience Queen," which is also the title of her solo book. Evie has overcome many personal challenges and obstacles in her life from physical, emotional and financial abuse, three divorces, a romance scam, the death of her parents, bullying and burnout. She has been an inspiration to many people of all ages, whether in training, education, mentoring and/or coaching.

After thirty-four years, Evie left the nursing and phlebotomy fields to become a businesswoman and vocational educator, trainer and assessor, helping countless students to fulfil their passion of becoming Phlebotomists. Having found her calling later in life, and after much soul searching, personal development, study in human psychology, Meta Dynamics and many other modalities, Evie became a life coach. Her specialty is in growth, embodiment and transformation, with a particular focus on health and relationships.

Chapter 2

My Fry Pan Moment

By Evie Csapo

I was almost thirty when my first husband disclosed he was having an affair in November of 1989.

We had been trying to have a baby, and we had agreed to get help to do this as my partner was infertile. It was right after our 6th visit to the fertility clinic. I recall hoping and praying for this one to be the lucky last time, but instead, he told me he was having an affair. Adding to that heartbreak, the insemination was unsuccessful. The betrayal cut like a knife. It crushed me. I walked out of a 10-year partnership with little to nothing, too upset and fragile to fight over possessions and money. It took me years and many tears to get over the heartbreak. I felt like such a failure, and to be honest, I was stuck playing the victim for many years to follow.

Late November 1992, mutual friends introduced me to who would become my second husband. He was tall, blue-eyed, charismatic with rugged good looks, an amazing Scottish accent, and funny to boot. We both brought emotional baggage into the relationship and faced many challenges. We married in 1995. Why? Because I thought that was the next phase of the relationship. We had a mortgage together and he liked the sound of boyfriend and girlfriend. He didn't want to marry; he was happy the way it was. The truth of the matter is that I was feeling insecure and wasn't listening to him or to my intuitive self. Only I didn't know this at the time. I ignored every red flag that was present. Instead, I walked on eggshells, and witnessed crazy acts of rage on the road and at home. He had black moods, depression, and paranoia. But as in most abusive relationships, we had fun between those awful times.

Throughout our ten years together, I tried to make him happy, and fix him. I had gained a little weight resulting in no intimacy, minimal affection, and I felt emotionally and physically abandoned. I decided to get fit and trim up. He was all for that and would make me fresh fruit juices to drink in the evenings. I amped up my exercise by walking everywhere. I lost my appetite and stopped eating. I also couldn't sleep and yet still had lots of energy. I was encouraged to keep drinking the fresh juice he made for me. I dropped two dress sizes in less than a month. He was still always angry, drunk and stoned. I was constantly stressed and emotional.

One day, I felt something inside of me snap. I felt trapped, controlled and so miserable. I literally had a breakdown. It took me two weeks to remember something as simple as my bank pin number or my own mobile number, and a month to fully recover. I was back to work by week five. The funny thing is we never discussed what happened to me. In fact, if I raised the topic, I would be stonewalled with, "It's over now. You're okay." Due to my feelings of shame and humiliation around the incident, I let it go too.

I told him I wanted to end our relationship. I didn't want to be with someone who was angry all the time, or someone who had me question where I stood in the relationship, or who put his addictive habits ahead of us as a couple. But then he promised he wanted to change, so we decided to give our marriage a second chance.

We went back home to Melbourne in August 1998, and for a year, it was bliss. We rented for a year, re-established our careers, and then got back into the property market at the end of 1999. Things began to change in 2000, when I stepped into a middle management position.

He had joined a local fire brigade and started hanging out with a woman that volunteered there, who he insisted was just a friend. Then the UGLY started again -- mood swings, rage, shouting, alcohol and drugs, and my disappointments, resentments, anger, pain, abandonment issues, and insecurities joined in the mix. It was toxic for both of us.

We went away for a weekend to Mt. Bogong with some people. We mountain biked down a trail on our way to The Rover Chalet. He took off like a cut snake. I took off fast at first, and quickly lost control. I hit my brakes too hard and fell off with the bike falling on top of me, landing on my right hip. I got straight back up, dusted myself off, and jumped back on my bike. The lads were laughing all the way down saying they've never seen anything like it, and that they'd still be sitting at the top of the mountain crying if it was them. The jokes eased my embarrassment and I laughed about it too. My husband wasn't concerned, even though I sported significant bruising. It slowed me down. I became the observer that weekend and noticed how dysfunctional he was with everyone at the chalet. I thought, *Oh my god, it's not just with me! He was angry with everyone.* He kept asking if the other woman from the brigade was coming. I began to suspect they were more than just friends.

My frypan moment came when we left Mt. Bogong to go home. He was driving recklessly down the mountain, and I was unsure why he was angry. As we got closer to Bright, we had phone service again. I got a message that a drunk driver had hit my mum at high speed. Later we established that the accident happened at the very same time I had crashed my mountain bike.

The trip away made me see that nothing had changed. I lost whatever remaining respect I had for him that weekend. I no longer loved him. I called this my Mt. Bogong Moment, but in fact the universe was hitting me over the head with a frypan. I couldn't do it anymore; I couldn't give anymore. I wasn't going to crash and fall again.

So, I told him I no longer wanted to be with him. He asked me why; I asked him what his ex-wife said when she broke it off, and he said, "She said, 'it's too hard, she couldn't do it anymore.'" So I said, "It's too hard, and I can't do this anymore." He thanked me for the best 10 years of his life, and said, "We sure had some fun."

It's May 2002, he moved out, and I was free. I spent a lot of time out with friends, long hours at work, went to gym three to four times a week, took up two dance classes, Salsa and Jive-n-Swing.

I power walked daily, mountain biked on weekends, went out dancing with my friends enjoying the single life, but I did not do the inner work on myself. I didn't do the healing. I vowed and declared I'd never allow anyone to shout, mistreat me, or physically or emotionally abuse me ever again. I kept myself so busy, and I was free to be me.

Fast forward to 2004. I had a health crisis with pneumonia, deep vein thrombosis in my left leg, and pulmonary embolisms in my lungs. I am an incredibly lucky woman to be here sharing this with you today. The consequences could have been catastrophic. It forced me to slow down. Advised by medico's to no longer do any contact sports, I felt like a ticking time bomb, unsure if I'd throw any more clots. So, I wrapped myself up in cotton candy and retreated from life for a year and half. I did not reach out to family or close friends for support.

It's July 2006, I'm now over just existing. I was 46 years old. I gathered my girlfriends together and we ventured off to New Zealand. We went to the Queenstown Winter Festival, where we all did something extreme. I learned how to snowboard at Coronet Peak over five days. I jumped out of a plane at 14,000 feet on a tandem skydive overlooking snow-capped mountains – ***all 4' 10" of me felt 6' tall and bulletproof!***

When I arrived home, I was so pumped and proud of myself for what I had accomplished. I decided it's time to get back out there and give internet dating a go. Rejection after rejection, mismatch after mismatch… It fuelled my lack of self-worth and self-doubt. Still, I persevered and then boom! I thought I'd hit the jackpot. I met a lovely gentleman who was funny and really into me.

He spoiled me with dinners out, flowers, dancing, beautiful sunset walks, country trips, and movies. We had so much fun. He showered me with attention, compliments and affection. I thought he was amazing. He was romantic and charming. He told me he had been bankrupt and shared what had happened in his past, as I did with him. He stated with conviction he would rebuild and would need five years to do so. I believed him.

Within three months he proposed. Within six months he moved into my house. It was a long engagement. I never had anyone nurture and care for me as much as he did. He was loving and attentive and couldn't do enough for me. After being on my own for so long, I lapped it up. He would call me six to ten times a day, if not more. He consumed my time. I didn't see it as controlling until later.

He kept borrowing money over and over and over and would never pay it back. Cracks started appearing. I would often discuss my concerns, but he would laugh it off or dismiss it. He would shut the conversation down and mock me. I asked him if he would contribute to the mortgage six weeks after he had moved in, and he told me in no uncertain terms that he wouldn't. If I expected him to pay board, he would go rent somewhere else.

It turned into a monster argument, and he never contributed to my mortgage in the eleven years he lived with me. Later in the relationship, in battles, he would tell me where the door was, and I would retaliate by stating the obvious, "It's my house, you leave." All that would do is give him more fuel to be angry, rude, punch walls, be disrespectful and shout at me. In the beginning I believed we could work out our differences.

Right there was my 'exit stage right' warning …. but no, I believed everyone deserved an opportunity to improve. I trusted him to do the right thing by us, by me.

Silly me!

We married in 2009. It was a beautiful wedding, all our friends and family attended. What people didn't know was that I paid for the wedding, the rings, the engagement party, and a 2008 holiday that was supposed to be paid back because it was a holiday he wanted for us. As a result, my savings was depleted, and my credit card almost maxed out. I had also re-mortgaged the house for more funds for his business.

Quite literally, the minute the ring went on my finger, things changed. We argued over everything. He was always angry or depressed, and I thought it meant he wasn't happy with me. I began trying to fix him. I wanted to help him. I also had my own stuff. I had already been married twice before. What would people think? What if I lose my house that I had worked so hard for?

On our first wedding anniversary, I recall wondering why we were not still in our honeymoon phase. Instead, we'd been in a constant battle over who was right or wrong. He knew me so well and would deliberately torment me, and he appeared when I felt hurt and upset.

I gave up the security of a full-time job in 2010 and went into business with my husband. I trusted that he would do the right thing by us. However, didn't understand the extent of his gambling addiction until we went into business together. There were many red flags, and I made so many excuses to cover up what I intuitively knew but did not want to believe. I had him painted as my soulmate, my best friend. I poured every cent I had into the business. It was meant to be ours, but it was his, and he wouldn't pay me a cent. I had no income coming in. I had to work a second job.

I worked hard for two years as a casual trainer, and even harder to have the opportunity to turn it into a full-time job, to escape working in the business with him. I couldn't believe it when I found out what he had been doing with the money. How could he do that? I felt so betrayed. I recall him throwing things at me and pushing me over in one of his many temper tantrums because I questioned him about his gambling.

I didn't realise just how much I had shut down. I had become numb and was in burnout due to the constant battles, financial and emotional abuse, lack of intimacy, sleep deprivation, and feeling trapped. I was not taking care of myself. I had given up and given in to my controlling, narcissistic, gambler husband. I had become a workaholic focusing on my career. I didn't recognise myself anymore.

I felt embarrassed and humiliated because my neighbours heard all our arguments. Trying to fight back and stand up to him while trying to salvage whatever pride was left, I still gave in to his demands for more money all the time. I'd feel guilty if I didn't help. I wanted to feel loved and wanted him to step up for me. Going from an athletic, fit, healthy size 8 to busting out of size 18's, it was the heaviest I had ever been in my entire life.

There was so much debt! We had three car loans, my house re-mortgaged many times, personal loans, maxed out credit cards, money owed to family, my superannuation raped, and no savings left for me to even runaway anymore. I asked, pleaded, and begged him to get a paid job, to get rid of the business, and seek support from professionals. The more I asked, the more he would dig his heels in and refuse. Nothing I said made any impact or even appeared to matter to him. Feeling unloved, undervalued, disrespected, and unattractive, I no longer trusted or respected him. He would threaten to kill himself whenever it looked like I was going to leave him. I was so unhappy.

I was living a dual life. To everyone else, work colleagues and friends, everything seemed okay. Although my boss would often see me change from happy to upset after every phone call I had with my husband. Sometimes my boss could hear him shouting at me through the phone for something that upset him. He was really loud.

One day, a colleague sat down on my desk and asked me if I was okay. Like a volcano, I erupted and shared all that was happening in the relationship. My colleague opened up a textbook and proceeded to show me the cycle of an abuser, and told me to leave when he was in the phase where he is on a high - the 'buying me flowers phase' - and get out of the abusive relationship. I recall saying, "I can't leave him. I'm his wife. I married him. I can't quit on him." She said, "Evie, you'll eventually have no choice. The universe will hit you on the head with a frypan."

That was in 2015. Being in denial, I refused to believe I could not save this marriage. I wanted the man I first met, not the man that showed up when he dropped his sheep's cloak. In early 2018, I called her and said, "It happened! The universe smashed me in the head with a frypan." I ended the relationship on December 8, 2017.

I was invited to a family function and my husband called me early in the day. He asked if I could leave work earlier than usual to get to his mum's first, where I was to change for the event. Only I didn't leave at 4:00 p.m. like I had planned. I finished at 4:35 p.m., just before he called. When I picked up the phone, he became abusive because I was late. I'm now stressed, concerned that he was in a bad mood, and angry at me… yet again. Taking off, I got to his mum's place with plenty of time to spare. His mum was upset because he had been shouting at her. It was so loud that a neighbour came down and told my husband he should be disgusted by how he spoke to his mother.

Not bothering to change, I went in my work wear, slacks and a shirt. We argued the whole way to the event. We arrived only to find out it was a formal event, long gowns, which he had failed to tell us. He did not speak to me the entire evening and sat at another table. I did my best not to show that I was upset.

On the way home he was trying his best to be pleasant to me. However, he was abusive, disrespectful, and rude to his mother, which continued when we arrived back at his mum's. Something inside me just snapped! What I saw in front of me was my life flash forward 20 years. Here was his 78-year-old mother still being abused and disrespected by this person, who stated how much he loved her.

I had just turned 58 years old and realised that nothing would change until I changed. So, **I chose ME**. I picked up my overnight bag and left. I told him that I was done and would be getting a divorce. I booked into a motel overnight and took off to visit family in central Victoria for the weekend, like I had done so many times before.

Coming back on Sunday, the 10th of August 2017, I got over the West Gate Bridge and was heading home, but something inside me said, *No way! You're not going back to that!* I decided that I needed to take care of myself. If I went back, it may be good for two weeks or so, and then it would go back to how it's always been. I had to take care of myself, and be there for my mum, as she was very sick and dying. Everything was changing. Life was happening now and it's precious.

A close friend of mine believed that my husband was a narcissist. This is what kick started my curiosity and healing journey. I wanted to know why I stayed in what was clearly not healthy for my mind, body and soul. First thing I did was discover what a narcissist was and began my awakening and soul journey back to my authentic self.

It was no longer about him, my past, or anyone else, it was all about me. I was still emotionally fragile. My mum was sick, and she was my confidante and my best friend. She had been diagnosed with three types of dementia, after being misdiagnosed with Parkinson disease. I felt very much alone, so when someone friended me on Instagram, I leaned in on my new friend. Everyone was busy with their own lives, and they did not see that I needed them. To me, the lack of support showed up as no one really cared anyway, even though I hadn't asked for help. Innocently, naively, and some may say, including myself, stupidly, I got myself caught in a web of lies, and I was the perfect victim for the romance scammer and/or catfish.

While I was at my most vulnerable, I was taken advantage of. I was groomed and manipulated. The scammer spoke with me the day my mother died; he spoke with my family. He hit me up for money, giving me a tragic story, and I believed him.

For the next twenty-two months, I helped people I had never met. I had only photos, phone calls, and text messages. For approximately 10 months, he stopped asking for financial help, therefore leading me into a false sense of security. We both leaned on each other for emotional support. We spoke about the possibilities of a future together.

In March 2020, he started asking for help and support again. Financially, things were extremely tough. I had little to no savings and struggled to make ends meet. I previously consolidated all the debts I inherited from my ex-husband and refinanced my home. However, due to inherited bad debt, my financial broker had secured me a low-doc loan at very high interest. It further complicated my financial health, helping a scammer/catfish. Any opportunity to have a healthy retirement, or keep my home was now gone. I felt I had no other option left; I had to sell. Again, I discussed this with the scammer, who I believed had my best interest at heart.

There are so many more details I could share about all that happened. However, at the end of the day, I made the choices rightly or wrongly. I discovered that whatever happened to me, does not define me, and has happened to many. I kept silent with every incident that ever happened to me in my life. That silence came from conditioning by my parents. I felt I never had a voice, I never felt heard, and now I have found my purpose. If I can help one person be more aware of their inner world before looking to the outside for validation, love, and acceptance, I've done my job.

What got me through it was by being curious about myself. I wanted to know why I thought more about others than I did of myself. I learned I was a fixer. I was a generous, loving, kind person to others and a mean girl to myself. There was a story constantly running that I was not good enough, not worthy enough. I was a failure, not good looking enough, too fat, too short, etc.

I brought my past into my future, finding reasons to validate the negative programming. Realising I lived in my stories, I would feel every emotion each time I retold them. I would relive every tragedy by telling my story over and over. I was stuck, and when I recognised and distinguished the difference between 'my stories' and 'what happened', my life changed. Now I focus on feedback and how I can continuously improve. *I am no longer the victim.*

My personal growth over the past four years has been exponential and I am continually learning and improving. I am a more radiant and confident version of my former self. I know my value, my worth and I am out to design my best life by living authentically true to myself. I can improve on my strengths and acknowledge myself for my courage and resilience. Rather than being the victim of circumstances, I choose to take action and steer my own boat instead of letting someone steer it for me. I see the growth and what I have taken away from the experiences is a greater awareness of who I am – a much wiser, more self-assured, confident, radiant soul who has great love to give.

What I discovered is this:

- I have always been very forgiving of others and have now learned how to forgive myself. I am aware that I am only human and make mistakes, but I am not perfect and that's okay!

- Resentment stops me from growing and keeps me stuck. Communicate and clear out what's in the way rather than let it build up.

- Bring my best self to everything. Don't look at mistakes as, *I am a failure*, but rather as feedback and an opportunity for growth.

- Resilience is key to overcoming challenges. Take the time needed to heal, then get back up, dust off and try, try again.

- SELF is valuable and important. Self-love, self-esteem, self-confidence and self-trust are keys to happiness. Take care of your mind, body and soul. My cup needs to runneth over, before I help others.

- Setting healthy, non-negotiable boundaries and knowing my worth are critically important.

- Make sure your wheel of life is balanced. Check it regularly. Access the areas in life that are important in order of priority, for example health & well-being, family, love and intimacy, career, spirituality, etc.

- Show up as my authentic self and do things to ensure personal growth and development is ongoing. Just like exercise, if I stop, I get out of shape. Do the inner work.

- Take notice of my feelings - If it doesn't feel good, safe or comfortable, don't do it. It has to make me feel good and give me the TINGLES.

- Sometimes it can be challenging to make changes, especially when I don't know what I don't know. That's why it's important to self-reflect, listen to my inner voice, trust my intuition, take courses and learn. Keep moving forward and take action to achieve my goals, dreams and desires.

- Trust that the universe always has my back; if I don't listen, she'll eventually hit me over the head with a frypan!

- I am important, and the only person that I can change is myself to be the best, greatest version of me that I can be.

- The greatest, best love ever is ME!

I found my precious mettle, giving me the ability to face challenging situations in a spirited and resilient way. I took the voyage to find my true essence and discovered my purpose. I am out to show you that it's never too late or too early to have, do or be whatever you want. I'm out to design my best life yet, showing up authentically for myself, and hopefully creating ripples of inspiration along the way.

It's all choice. It's your choice. Do you have the METTLE to dive deeply to find your precious authentic self?

My resilience and experience have allowed my passion and purpose to emerge. As a result, I am an intuitive growth, embodiment and transformational leader and life coach, inspiring and supporting people to reach their full potential. I will hold you accountable for reaching your goals, and help you build and design a bridge to attain your dreams, vision, and mission without getting stuck at the bottom of the cliff and trying to climb back out on your own.

Trust the universe has your back, and if you still miss the signs along the way, know that you too may have a frypan moment.

Just be ready for it!

Glow like Magic,

Evie X

LINDA HO

Linda Ho is a beautiful soul living in New Zealand. She has travelled around the world and has lived in multiple countries. Fascinated with the power of the mind, Linda's journey started on her own healing quest. After many years of trial and error, she was introduced to ancient and modern tools. She learned how to heal herself and break old family patterns, which allowed her to create her dream life. Now she uses those tools to help her clients heal and become who they truly are.

If you get a chance to meet her, Linda will tell you that deep within you is a gift waiting to be unlocked. She believes you can have it all, and your mind is the only thing standing between you and your dreams.

Linda is the founder of the Abundant Goddess Club. She serves women worldwide, helping them create a life of their own design using their feminine energy.

Get your FREE gift from Linda: www.lindaspecialgift.com.

Chapter 3

The Universe Burned My Lifeboats

by Linda Ho

It all started at the beginning of 2021. We were living in Mount Maunganui, New Zealand. I had made good friends, and we started getting to know the neighbours. After moving so many times, we finally found a nice place to settle. It had been a year of chaos, lockdowns and uncertainty, but there were many benefits too. It brought us closer to ourselves, our marriage and our children as we spent a lot of time together and worked through every upcoming challenge together.

Beginning in 2021, we received an email from the property management company that our contract was ending. We assumed we would be on a loose contract, so we weren't too concerned about leaving. However, through Covid, the couple who owned the house got divorced, and sold the house. The new owners had plans to keep this house as a holiday house. We assumed they would want us out after winter so they could enjoy the place in summer, as it is a desired holiday destination with beautiful white beaches and a big mountain to climb with the most magnificent view.

Then my phone rang, and it was the property manager. I asked her about our contract. She asked, "Did you not get my email?" I replied, "Yes, we did … Joe read it and mentioned that the contract is coming to an end." She answered, "No, no, no, they want you to be OUT!"

I could feel my blood drop, and the colour fade from my face. I was completely in shock. It was only two more weeks until the contract was running out, and we hadn't looked for anything. We had no place lined up, nowhere to go, and a whole house worth of stuff to store.

She said she could call them and ask if they would give us more time.

I called Joe and said, "I thought you read the email… they want us to be out!". I was devasted and soooo stressed and angry at Joe for misinterpreting it so badly!

We started looking for rental properties and instantly got six declines. We were concerned and felt something must be wrong. People love us. We are the perfect tenants. We are both health professionals. I run my business as a spiritual mindset coach. Who wouldn't want us to be in their house?

I asked Joe if he had mentioned that we went to tribunal. He confirmed, saying it was one of the questions on the application process. Our previous property manager was the worst! She tried to bully us out of our bond. Since we owned two properties ourselves, we knew the law and didn't allow her to walk all over us. In court, the judge agreed with us, and she ended up getting nothing. Nevertheless, this became a stain on our rental applications and prevented us from getting a property.

I was worried sick. I recently started a new job as a Practice Nurse Team Leader, and I had only been working there for a few months. We looked for a house to buy but nothing seemed to land at that time.

A few days in, Joe called me and said he found a way to store all of our stuff. It's super cheap and the company can ship the container wherever we want to move. I was relieved! At least that's sorted out. We talked about what we should do and where we should go. We decided to stay with his family back in Auckland until we figured things out.

Then I thought, *why aren't we checking out the South Island?* We heard that the landscape is magnificent, and houses are much cheaper down there. So, we packed the children in the car and drove down to check out the South Island. As soon as we arrived on the island, you could feel the energy change and things started to slow down. It felt great.

We decided we would move somewhere south. So, both of us handed in our resignations and started to look for a place we could call home. We drove to Picton, Blenheim, Kaikoura and all the way to Christchurch. We almost bought a piece of land between Kaikoura and Cheviot. It was a stunning beachfront. Dolphins were always there, and a big seal hanging out in front of the property… what a dream!

We called our lawyer to get the sales agreement ready. Then someone snapped it up in front of our eyes! The owner didn't even want to negotiate with us and literally just said, "No thanks. Goodbye." We were shocked! No one had made an offer for a year; we were the first. That was so weird. Who could have snapped it from us? After some thought, we agreed that everything happens for a reason, and maybe this protected us from our kids drowning in the sea as it wasn't a swimmable beach. We were devastated. We already started to fantasise about what it would be like living there.

We finally moved out of the house, and Joe took the kids to his parents. I had to work two more weeks to honour my notice period. At that time, a lot of people were telling me about Nelson and Golden Bay. So, Joe and I met in Nelson. We planned a little holiday there while we looked for our perfect home. We checked out the properties on the platform *Trademe* and found a few we thought we'd enjoy.

We saw a few places up in Golden Bay, a two-hour drive away from Nelson. It had beautiful beaches, mountains, bush, anything you can imagine. Golden Bay was beautiful! However, every house we liked was on the last day of tender, so we had to make some quick decisions. We made an offer on a few houses, but they weren't accepted. So, our search for that perfect home continued. We came back to Nelson and stayed for ten days at a hotel on the beach, close to the park and playgrounds.

We continued to do our research and finally found a house. It was perfect! It had ocean views, a big pool and indoor spa. I was in love with it! It needed some updating, but it had amazing potential.

We made an offer, and it was accepted. The old couple who lived there wanted a three-month settlement to have enough time to move out. We only had two weeks to find jobs, so that the banks would approve our loan. It was crazy.

We called our old employers and asked them if we could work there for six months or more. We needed to stay in Auckland while the house was being renovated. Thankfully, we both found jobs. It felt like this was meant to be because it all went smooth and easy. We were so stoked for things finally flowing our way.

After six months, we were planning our move to our new home. It was so exciting. Finally, all our dreams were coming true. Joe landed a great job with the possibility of becoming a partner. I decided to wait until we got to Nelson.

We found out that one of my friends was also moving to Nelson. Her daughter was the same age as mine, so it seemed like everything was perfect. Instantly, we had some friends, my daughter had a friend, and Joe already had a job. It felt so right.

Once we were in Nelson, I got a job as Clinical Nurse Manager. I was thrilled! I thought it would be a nice way to finish my career. Then I'd focus on my spiritual mindset and abundance coaching. I loved my team, everyone in the office was amazing, and I had a great boss. It was a beautiful place to work.

In the background, COVID was still a thing, and they started to roll out the vaccines. I had some bad experiences with vaccines, so I knew I wasn't getting it anytime soon. I wanted to wait to see long term results. Unfortunately, that wasn't possible because they announced that all teachers and health professionals had to get the vaccine in order to keep their jobs.

I was shocked, but at the same time, a wave of relief washed over me. The universe/God was burning my boats. I had always kept nursing in my back pocket and, as a result, I never went all in on my business. I knew now there was no way back unless I got the jab.

As I learned more about the vaccines, I was convinced not to get it, knowing that my body would handle the actual disease much better than the shot. This meant that I had to say goodbye to nursing forever. However, I honoured my beliefs and did what I felt was right for me and my family.

Eventually, we moved to Golden Bay, where we initially looked for a place to live. We found a beautiful property with ocean views, lots of fruit trees and land. My husband's parents ended up moving here too. We're so grateful to have them nearby.

It is here, in Golden Bay, that I have launched my coaching business. I teach online and have half-day workshops and retreats. I use Neuro-Linguistic Programming, Time Line Therapy™, Transformational Breathwork and other techniques to help women across the globe awaken to their power and become abundant Goddesses!

Lisa Jowett

When Lisa Jowett decided to become a personal trainer at the age of forty, everyone thought she was crazy. It was the best career decision Lisa ever made! She became a health and fitness coach, international business coach and proud owner of Busy Bods, and Mind Body Warriors.

Lisa is passionate about helping women find happiness and feel good about who they are by becoming the best versions of themselves through fitness, nutrition, and mindset.

She also has a burning desire to help other coaches launch and grow their businesses.

One of Lisa's core beliefs is that a healthy lifestyle is much more than lifting weights. It's about focusing on a positive body image, stretching, de-stressing, healthy eating, and getting rest and enough sleep. She loves helping others see and experience what their bodies are capable of. Lisa makes it a goal to help them achieve a happy and well-balanced lifestyle that will minimise the risk of future health-related issues.

Chapter 4

The Magic of Your Heart

by Lisa Jowett

"What? You're going to become a personal trainer, Lisa? You're almost forty!"

Unfortunately, this was the common response when I told my friends and family that I wanted to become a personal trainer. They were genuinely concerned that nobody would want to train with someone so old. Not to mention most personal trainers only last six to twelve months in the industry.

At the time, I felt disappointed by the initial lack of support, but I didn't let it stop me because once I decide to do something, I'm going to do it!

Now I look back on those conversations and understand why they had their concerns. I know they genuinely had my best interest at heart, but they didn't know what my motivation was because I'd never explained it to them.

As a kid, I was really active. I played competitive netball, tennis, softball, swam and danced. In my teens and early twenties, I chose clubbing and bands over sports. I did train at the gym, but let's face it I was burning some serious calories on those dance floors!

At twenty-six, I had my first baby, Jake, and three years later I had Elisha. At the time, my focus was on my family and work. I would throw in some exercise here and there, but I never committed to anything for any length of time because I would always feel guilty putting myself first. I now know how wrong my mindset was.

Almost ten years ago, I left my volatile marriage. For eight months or so, until we got back on our feet, we stayed with my parents or our friends, Tracey and Greg. I was welcome to stay with many other friends who offered me their lounges and spare rooms, like Deb, Samera, and Tiff, to name a few. I never thought I'd be couch surfing at the age of 38, but there I was, getting around like a gypsy.

I was in survival mode. It was disruptive, and I was in the trenches, but I was ok with it because I had the support of many kind-hearted loved ones, and I am forever grateful.

We finally sold our home, and my kids and I moved into an apartment. I was extremely happy to be starting my new life, but there were the stresses of being a single, full-time mum due to my kids' dad moving overseas for over three years.

I was working full-time at Pacific Publishing in the inner city. I was busier than ever, causing me to feel stressed. Without fail, I woke up every morning around 3 a.m. gasping for air. I felt like I was dying. The anxiety I was feeling was starting to take its toll on me. I was exhausted and didn't feel like myself. I wasn't keen on taking meds, so I decided to try a more holistic approach.

I chose to put all my efforts into getting my health into order because I knew how good exercise made me feel as a kid. I started jogging at 5 a.m. every morning while my kids were sleeping. Not long after, I joined a gym where I would train every morning without fail. I eliminated processed food, lowered my alcohol consumption, focused on being positive, and eventually, the anxiety began to ease.

My early morning runs and training at the gym with a personal trainer (PT) got me through the most challenging time of my life. Before I knew it, I was giving friends and colleagues health and fitness advice. I loved helping people, and after experiencing the benefits of my lifestyle changes, I decided I wanted to change careers so I could help other people experience it too.

I decided to study fitness at FIA Fitnation. They offered online classes and a mix of face-to-face and online classes. I hadn't studied in many years, so I was worried about my learning capabilities and opted for the mix. Unfortunately, the only day I could take classes was on Saturday due to work commitments. As one can imagine, the old mama guilt started to kick in. Although it's not a degree (far from it), I still had to sacrifice time away from my kids, which concerned me because weekends were the only opportunity to get quality time with them.

After thinking about what I really wanted for my future, I decided to start the course. I had the support of my parents and friends, who helped me with my kids, and I am forever thankful.

A couple of years later, my journey into the coaching world commenced. My first gig was teaching bootcamp classes before work for my friend Troy. Then I worked full-time for Virgin Active for over three years. Three years ago, I started my own personal training business called "BusyBods."

In 2014, I met my soulmate Gregg on Tinder (again, many thought this was a bad idea), and in all fairness, I didn't expect to fall in love again. But, to my surprise, I did, and we married in 2019. Gregg owns a construction business and has been an entrepreneur for most of his working life. Honestly, I don't think I would have taken the plunge as a business owner if it hadn't been for his unbelievable support.

Gregg and I are a great match. He is the risk taker, and I'm risk averse, but we are both open to suggestions. Together, we take calculated risks, which has helped both our businesses boom. I truly feel so blessed to have met such a wonderful man, especially online. Who would have thought?

I'm incredibly indebted for all the doors which have opened for me since making the scary decision to change careers at the ripe old age of forty! Of course, I am joking about forty being old. Age is just a number, and we can do whatever our heart desires at any age.

My first taste into the fitness industry was thanks to my friend, Troy, who asked me to teach some of his bootcamp classes at Centennial Park. It was the perfect part-time gig that gave me some industry experience.

Not long after, I accepted a job at Virgin Active at Moore Park as a Fitness Pro, until I scaled my own personal training business.

Thanks to the great training and the wonderful trainers who surrounded me, I learned so much at Virgin. I loved my job. I had incredible clients who are now my friends. I followed my heart, and now I'm helping people, just like I wanted to.

At this point, I have trained hundreds of women and some men, which has given me an unbelievable amount of job satisfaction. I have helped my clients drop kilos, build muscle, increase their energy and build confidence. I have been able to help clients get off anti-depressants, anti-anxiety meds, lower their blood pressure and reverse Type 2 Diabetes. It's an unimaginable feeling knowing that I have been able to help my clients make healthy sustainable lifestyle choices which will add years to their lives. As a disclaimer, I do not give medical advice and am not a physician. I strongly recommend that everyone be under the care of a physician before engaging in any physical training.

Mid 2019, I started my own mobile PT business BusyBods. I knew how to train people but had no idea how to run a business! I thought I'd simply join a couple of mum's groups on Facebook, and it would be smooth sailing. Boy was I wrong! My first six months were pretty slow. I was conducting about twelve to fifteen sessions per week, helping me pay my bills, but not much else. In 2020, I started to build momentum, but then you guessed it, Covid hit, and Sydney had its first lockdown!

I was legally allowed to train my clients because most of my sessions were one-on-one. However, some of my clients started worrying about the virus and decided to go into their own lockdowns. I took my business online and loaned out the majority of my equipment to my clients, so they didn't just have to do bodyweight exercises.

This was my first introduction to the virtual training world, and my clients soon realised I could work them just as hard! I enjoyed having the freedom to work from home. I could see the potential, so I decided I would run some Facebook advertisements to gain some more clients. A few leads came in but none of them became clients, so I was disappointed. However, I wasn't too worried because Sydney was opening up again.

I started seeing my clients face-to-face again, and my business was growing. However, in the back of my mind, I was concerned that there would be another lockdown because Covid certainly wasn't going away!

Towards the end of 2020, I decided it was time to hire a business coach to help me gain online clients. I loved my face-to-face clients, but I wanted to future-proof my business and felt the only way would be to get into the online space.

I chatted with a few different coaches, but none quite had the expertise I was after until I met Jason Grossman, the founder of Quantum Business Coaching. Jason was originally a PT who had worked at several gyms and owned his own. He pushed me out of my comfort zone and had me doing things I never thought possible! I liked writing blogs, but the thought of talking on camera scared the crap out of me. Before I knew it, I was doing regular livestreams, running webinars, doing challenges and workshops and getting featured on a podcasts.

My business was starting to boom, and the timing was divine because Sydney went into a four-month lockdown not long after!

Sadly, other businesses were shutting down, and I felt so sorry for them. However, I was thankful that I had pivoted into the online space, and 2021 was my best financial year to date!

Jason was so impressed with my business success that he offered me a part-time role as a business coach. I couldn't believe he had asked me, but I was thrilled. I accepted his offer even though I didn't think I was ready for it. One of the great things about having a coach is they will see your potential before you do and move you forward at an accelerated pace.

You're probably thinking, why would I take on this role when my business was doing so well? Please let me explain. I love helping people and I wanted to give back. After all, as mentioned earlier in this chapter, most PTs in the industry only last six to twelve months due to their lack of business and marketing skills. So, I want to help them succeed. Not to mention, for the rest of my life, I want to continually develop my skills and take on different projects if they are the right fit for me.

I truly believe that things happen for a reason in your life, but you must be open-minded, or you'll blink and miss it.

In 2021, I helped more women and men on their health and fitness journeys than ever before. I have made many new friendships with people from all over the world, and met my new business partner, Kate Southall, who is also featured in this book.

Kate joined my 21-day online challenge, and not long after, I personally trained her. Kate is a life and business coach, and we hit it off like a house on fire. You know when you meet someone, and you just 'get' each other? This was us, and before long, we were doing webinars together. In 2022, we will be launching a joint venture called Mind Body Warriors.

Over the years, Kate and I discovered that many ambitious mamas have dedicated all their time to their careers and families but have put their needs last. We recognise it in ourselves too. While it appears to be commendable to the outside world, these burned-out mums are tired, unfit, have health problems, and are looking for a change.

Kate and I felt there was a gap in the market. We are both super excited to be launching a program like no other which will include mindset, nutrition, fitness, getaways, adventures, relaxation, fun and more. We both truly believe that if we live our ultimate life, we need all pillars to align.

To my surprise, 2021 was my greatest year for opportunities and growth, but it wasn't easy. I felt very uncomfortable, and there were many times that my anxiety kicked in, and I felt like giving up. But I learned how to get comfortable with being uncomfortable; after all, this is the only way I can grow.

I could never have imagined in my wildest dreams that my life would take this path after following my heart and taking a risk. However, I believe that you will be successful if you are truly passionate and invested in your dream.

Times have changed and gone are the days when you only have one career in your lifetime. I'm glad they have because there is a big difference between starting a new career as a forty-year-old compared to when I began my first career.

I was only sixteen when I got into the world of magazines, and while I loved my job, it wasn't my heart-centred desire. I was more interested in the social life and the partying side, to be honest with you. Not to mention, I grew up in a middle-class family in the suburbs of Sydney. I lived a reasonably sheltered life, so I wasn't fully prepared for what life had to offer.

Fast forward to forty, and I was a totally different person. I had many life experiences and had gone through some really tough times leading me to change careers. My heart and mind connected, and I finally knew what I wanted out of life. I found my purpose to help others and make a difference in the world.

I truly believe that everything in life happens for a reason, the good, the bad, and the ugly. My past has shaped me to be the person I am today. I had to experience some hardship in my life, and I feel I should thank my ex-husband for that because my life now has so much more purpose.

You only get one life, and I know that many people have great ideas. However, unfortunately for the majority, they won't ever act on it because they fear failure. Trust me, I know, because I was that exact person until I was forty! You shouldn't be surprised though. After all, it is ingrained in you from an early age. You're taught not to take risks or make mistakes at school. It's all about getting the best grades. However, in the real world, the people who are willing to give it a go, and learn from their mistakes, are generally the most successful.

While my journey has been a roller coaster, there have been many tears, sleepless nights, and plenty of self-doubts. However, I have always kept my eye on the prize, which is to help as many people as humanly possible as they embark on their health and fitness journeys and business ventures.

LINH LE

Linh Le is a highly sought-after Senior Leading Teacher and Family Coach with over twenty years of experience working with children, adults, and teachers. She is passionate about helping families thrive through constructive communication, genuine trust, and sincere appreciation of one another.

Once a strict mother, who led her sons to academic and musical excellence, she learned first-hand the pain her vigilance brought to her family members. As a result of her quest to heal herself, she discovered powerful tools, techniques and strategies that have significantly improved her family dynamics.

Linh is a local celebrity, appearing on the Family Happiness segment on the Australian SBS Vietnamese radio station.

Connect with Family Coach Linh Le for a Free 5 Steps to Creating Deeper Connection eBook.

Facebook: https://www.facebook.com/LinhLeFamilyCoach

Email: linh@linhlecoaching.com

Chapter 5

The Silent Whisper of the 'Good Mother'

By Linh Le

Five years ago, in 2017, I made a conscious decision to… let go. Resigned from being a good mother, I was a helicopter mum sometimes, hovering over everything my boys did. Other times, a real tiger mum, setting high standards and expectations. Super organised and active every moment of the day, I was hyper focused. We were high achievers with scholarships and selective school offerings, music recognitions, sports captaincy, house captaincy and community leadership roles.

I am forever grateful for the experiences we've had and the success we've achieved. While we are many years away from that world of 'controlled parenting' now, I must admit, for a long time, I've had to wrestle with a vigorous internal battle of guilt, confusion and self-doubts.

This is my story of being a vigilant mother with her capable team, my loving, super supportive husband and two diligent boys. They are three and a half years apart. We were excited for a journey full of joy, love, success, harmony, fulfilment and everything beautiful promised to a happy family. Instead, we found ourselves in total chaos full of emptiness, anger, frustration, fear, blame, defence and helplessness.

Then came the whisper…

Yes, two years before this radical decision, in February 2015, we sat in the headmaster's office of one of Melbourne's most prestigious grammar schools to receive my eldest son, Jordan's, scholarship award. We were proud and so happy! Mission accomplished, you might say.

In that moment, a helpless cry for attention awakened in me - a whisper like none other.

Unfortunately, the whisper was drowned out by the drive and determination to stay focused and continue moving ahead.

Have you ever been so focused on something that you see, hear, and feel nothing else? Like a horse on a busy suburban street, each eye covered, she has only one thing to do, and that is to stay focused on pulling the heavy carriage ahead. Regardless of the pain or pleasure, she does what she has to do.

I had a miscarriage before, so I have been very vigilant with Jordan from day one. He was a fine baby, 'perfect' in every way. He ate well, slept well, looked beautiful, was cheerful, lively, and easy to teach. He was receptive, and I was happy to teach. By the young age of three, Jordan had learned the alphabet and read fluently before starting school. He also had years of experience with music, swimming, martial arts and sports, which was a pat on the back for me, the amazing, devoted mother. I was proud, and I felt validated.

Leigh, my second born, was physically the same but feisty in nature. He lived passionately and was a natural entertainer the moment he could walk. He would dance and draw for hours on end and do more if he was given the chance. But getting him to focus on anything else was always a challenge. However, being as vigilant as I was, consider it done. Leigh knew the alphabet before he turned three.

Leigh spent two years of kinder and school and still didn't know the four basic 2D shapes; He was never interested in anything academic. Squares, circles, rectangles and triangles were irrelevant to his love for music and performing. I was mortified when I noticed this and upped my level of intensity and focus.

Within a month, Leigh knew the shapes but had fallen behind his peers in reading. Again, I got focused, and he moved up ten levels within one school term, joining the top reading group. Every child can learn. It's only a matter of focus. While this belief remains true to me, I was missing one fundamental awareness, the consideration for the willingness of their heart.

Like many of us, I wanted to make life as easy as possible for my kids. My parental responsibility was to do what I could to remove the pains of life and provide them with opportunities. Little did I know, this led the whole family far from the joy of life and directly to disconnection. We became disconnected from ourselves, and eventually became disconnected from one another.

The pain was like no other. Slowly it played out, painfully stinging our hearts, so silently, so unclear. Within a few years, it eroded our love for ourselves and our passion for life.

Gabor Mate' is a highly respected Hungarian physician who has a special interest in childhood development and trauma. In an interview, he shared his mentor's formulation on trauma…

"The biggest loss is the connection to ourselves."

Working full-time meant I had to stay focused on the goals. My family deserves my 'best' effort. So, I did my very best to keep us on a regimented schedule. We had lists of activities to tick off, long drives between activities to learn from the best teachers, meals in the car, and homework on vacations. Regrettably, my best was not without shouting episodes that were not aligned with love, care and respect. I began to control their every minute; 'no' was never an acceptable answer. Soon I was very unpleasant to be around. And eventually, we lost the warm fuzzy feelings in our embrace. The death of connection.

I was so time-poor. My interactions with extended family and friends were limited. I was not present to them and their feelings, which hurt our relationships and brought distance between us. Some are irreconcilable to this day. Eventually, for me, life became a relentless cycle of schedules, and directed activities focused on chasing an abstract goal of raising 'happy and successful' children and being a 'good' mum. The irony was that the harder I tried, the further away I was from achieving it.

"Your job is less to instil curiosity in your kids than to make sure you don't squash what is already there." Neil deGrasse Tyson - Astrophysicist

I was on a quest to *prepare* Jordan and Leigh for a fulfilled life. Completely missing their individual voices. It took me a long time to recognise and admit that I had *my best interest* at heart, not theirs. I was making sure I was a good mother, a role to fulfil, not a relationship to develop and nurture.

One of my clients courageously shared a reflection of his parenting style in our parenting community. He said, "When I look after my sixteen-month-old daughter, I try to manage her, the dishes and tidying up the house simultaneously. It looked like I was doing my best to be the best dad for her and the family but what I really wanted was time for myself as soon as we put her into bed. I often missed my chance to connect with her and for her to connect with me."

Jordan was a high achiever; he had many achievements in sports and was involved in the community. He also played the piano and composed musical pieces using multiple instruments. Some were quality enough for Yamaha International competitions. He also played the cello and the trombone. He was the pride of the family. Grandpa, my husband's father, had every hope that both of us would brighten the 'face' of the family.

"He is a natural." his teachers assured me.

Unfortunately, by the time Jordan reached eleventh-grade, he had given everything up, including his will to work hard academically. No matter how much attention and praise he received from teachers, friends and family, external validations were not enough. Quite the contrary. Jordan later revealed that they only added to the pressure. The help that I gave him to achieve so much took away his sense of freedom. "It didn't matter what I could do or what I achieved. I was never myself."

Jordan's and Leigh's reluctance to follow my lead made my endeavour to create well-rounded children exhausting. It was a real problem. I knew something needed to change. Surely, we all deserve a life that we love living.

Albert Einstein once said, "We cannot solve our problems with the same thinking we used when we created them." However, I didn't know what that meant! I was clouded by fear and confusion. How do I change my thinking? If I don't continue, my children will surely fall behind. That would be irresponsible! I must be crazy to throw it all away now with everything we've been through! And it might seem unbelievable, but I really thought I was going crazy. Crazy to even entertain the thoughts that there might be another way of 'good' parenting. So, I told myself that I just needed some rest. Take a breather, So I did. I took a deep breath, stayed busy, and continued to lead the family team as I always have. I was aching and dying inside, ignoring the echo of that silent whisper for change.

From then on, I became more observant. We went on vacation overseas, and we brought Leigh's French horn along. We didn't want him to miss a day of practice because he was applying for The Victorian College of the Arts Secondary School (VCASS). We made sure he practised every day, which paid off because he got an offer to join the school. Once again, I succeeded as a skillful mother. However, this time I did not feel validated. I noticed, at the age of twelve, the once energetic child had become submissive to my regiment. I won. He lost his will to push against me, and so too, he lost his passion for life.

Jordan's body language said it all. His shoulders began to sag. The once happy, confident child was now afraid of everything, particularly of making decisions. He was petrified of making mistakes and was totally unsure of himself.

Les Brown said, "The graveyard is the richest place on Earth because it is here that you will find all the hopes and dreams that were never fulfilled, the books that were never written, the songs that were never sung, the inventions that were never shared, the cures that were never discovered, all because someone was too afraid to take that first step, keep with the problem, or determined to carry out their dream."

My family was not fulfilled. My husband complained that he did not think parenting would be "like this". When he came home after work, he was usually greeted with complaints about the kids and accusations instead of warm smiles and tight cuddles. So disconnected, both of us began to experience symptoms of depression.

We blamed our despair on a midlife crisis. We were both in our early forties. So, it was only natural that we would feel miserable. Absurd, but we did think that.

Jordan showed more resistance. He was always grumpy and reluctant to show up to his music classes. We made excuses for him thinking, 'all teens are like that! He'll grow out of it.'

Unfortunately, they don't.

When well-intentioned parents refuse to listen to their kids' cries for help, it can have devastating consequences. Feeling unseen can affect their self-esteem, sense of self-worth, and so much more. So, it's important to deal with it right away. Otherwise, it will need to be addressed later in life.

For Leigh, we blamed him because he can be *very stubborn*. How convenient, or rather inconvenient, that we can always find a reason not to deal with our issues.

One day, while dropping Jordan off at a music class, he burst into tears and shouted, "I hate all my teachers! Mum, you don't know how hard my life is."

Jordan was in deep pain and felt helpless.

The whisper became a roar. It was loud and clear.

Don't wait until you find another way!

Stop!

Now!

Another way was finally revealed. No, it was shoved in my face! It said that I needed to get help.

The next morning, I went to the school's psychologist's office. I intended to find help for Jordan. But, to be honest, I think I was looking for a way to blame the school and teachers for my child feeling so much pain. I knew Jordan didn't hate his teachers. I knew it was something else that was causing the pain.

After a 45-minute chat, I knew what it was when I found myself cupping my tear-stained face wishing for a parenting manual. I realised I was completely lost on this journey. I didn't know how to parent effectively. Nothing made sense anymore. The long walk from the school's gate to my car gave me time to accept what was opened for me.

Instead of feeling sorry for myself and riddled with regret, I felt light and clear. As if I had been holding my breath underwater and finally resurfaced for deliciously clear air. I let go of the assumption that being a good mother should come naturally because I was a teacher. I admitted that I didn't know the best way to parent my children, and that I needed help. I felt a release, like a gentle breeze, when I did this. The dark clouds hanging over my head disappeared. Yes! I surrendered!

The invisible chains that anchored me to the depth of a relentlessly raging sea of expectations and approvals broke loose when I accepted that I didn't know everything, and I needed help. That said, I didn't know where to get the help. So, I educated myself by watching YouTube videos, listening to podcasts, reading books, enrolling in courses and seminars, and finding a coach. 'Changing my thinking'... thank you Mr. Einstein!

The Change

My parenting journey was confusing, to say the least. I was oscillating between controlling everything and trusting that my children could find their own way. I struggled with my inner thoughts and conflicts. The question of what is right and what is wrong tormented me. Every bad grade, every missed opportunity, every time someone else's kids had an achievement, I would question myself.

My family was like some lost rabbits bouncing from one rabbit hole to another, not knowing exactly where home was. One moment, Mum expected everything in order - 'do as I say'. And another moment, it was a free for all 'make your own decisions, don't ask me'. I was still haunted by the belief that things would be different if I was better, smarter, and worked harder. But each time I began to hover, I was not at peace with the person I was becoming- controlling, unpleasant and absent.

So, I continued to search for *another way*.

Eventually, one inner battle after another, I learned to dance with my fears and broke through my need for control. I learned to handle myself with each mistake and each disappointment. I slowly accepted myself and my weaknesses. I slowly let go of control and allowed a new kind of relationship to sprout. Soon, the kids labelled me as 'Old Mum' and 'New Mum'.

The laughter and acceptance returned, and love and connection were truly present. Harmony is possible among the most obvious differences. I made my way back to my abandoned heart and, eventually, allowed everyone else in the family to find their way back to theirs.

Everything began to fall into place, depression symptoms disappeared, and shoulders straightened up. We began to have deep, intimate conversations. Dreams were finding their way back, and independence began to sprout. Our family relationships deepened, especially between Leigh and Jordan.

I released my grip, and the boys took control of their schooling and achievements. They were learning lessons they would never have learned if I was still hovering over them. Jordan made some poor decisions, yes, and he learned from them. He realised that the world continues to spin, and it only matters what he chooses to do next. He is happy to have the freedom to craft his life one decision at a time.

Leigh is fifteen, and adolescent years come with their challenges. He has spent many nights crying to Mum, sharing his pain and experiences, while I stayed silent and present to his feelings. I offer my help but leave the choice entirely to him, allowing him to live his own life.

I now spend less time scheduling and dishing out reminders, painting scary future scenarios, and hovering over them to ensure things happen the 'right' way. Now, my husband and I have more time for each other. We bravely embark in deeper communications, allowing us to heal which brings us to a higher level of love and appreciation for one another.

I am obsessed with understanding human behaviours and the dance between our internal and external worlds. As a result of my experiences parenting my two sons, I have designed courses and programs to empower parents. My programs facilitate growth and deepen family connections. I am pleased to be a leader in a community that believes there is another way of parenting. A parenting style that allows us to nurture the essence of a child; where joy, harmony and success can exist to create that sense of fulfilment in every family member.

If you are yet to be convinced that being a good parent means having a strong connection to yourself first, then here's another quote from the wisdoms that have lived on for centuries.

"The most important thing is relationships. Without understanding relationships, any plan of action would only breed conflict." Krishna Morty

And to me, the best place to start is in the interactions we have with our family… those closest to our heart. Here I've recognised that there was a conflict between my inner world and my external world. The way I viewed my role as a 'good' mother was not aligned with my values and my children's needs.

We are all different and unique, but we allow our inner guidance to be drowned out by others, such as culture, traditions, and society etc., causing us to feel lost and empty. But, it is never too late to listen to the whispers of your heart. No matter how far away you think you are from your truth or how old your children are, no matter how hard you've tried to connect and feel 'at one' with life…remember, you always got your inner world.

Do you hear the whisper of your heart? Or that of your children calling out to you?

Like me, you may have left them behind unknowingly. Your heart is waiting. Your children's hearts are waiting. Regardless of what we think, the connection between a child and a parent is one to be cherished. If you feel disconnected, I encourage you to find your personal path to reconnect with yourself and your loved ones. I promise you, it will be rewarding and well worth the effort.

I want to share another great quote from Albert Einstein, "The measure of intelligence is the ability to change."

Change is hard but possible and waking up to the truth within you is to return home. Come home. There is a warm loving you waiting and longing for your return.

There is a path available to you so you can return home. You simply need someone to light that path and help you find your way. Once you do, you'll be able to help your children find their way too. Each family member will be loving and living true to who they are.

There is one more quote I'd like to share with you, which is from The Dalai Lama.

"Man surprised me most about humanity. Because he sacrifices his health in order to make money. Then he sacrifices money to recuperate his health. And then he is so anxious about the future; he lives as if he is never going to die, and then dies having never really lived."

If you would like someone to guide you and help you find your way, please connect.

Love,

Linh Le

Championing Your Family Connections.

CARMEN LOUISE

Carmen Louise is an adoring mother and partner who owns a Martial Arts Centre called Exclusive Fitness and Martial Arts and has launched Worldly Women in Martial Arts (WWMA). She was cast as the first and only female of "Warrior Gene" for Season 1, a documentary about Martial Arts Coaches.

Carmen has an impressive list of martial arts achievements, including obtaining her black belt 3rd degree in Karate and receiving her BJJ brown belt after winning gold at the Victorian State Championships. She was also invited by the Australian Institute of Sport to train with the Rio Olympic team.

Carmen navigates life with Ehlers Danlos Syndrome, a connective tissue disorder she's had since she was born. She was also born to the hands of a severely abusive father. She truly believes that if she can endure all that she has and ultimately live her dream life, then others can too. Leading by example and sharing her authentic truths, Carmen became a Martial Arts self-defense specialist to teach people how to protect themselves and build their self-worth.

Chapter 6

Silver Linings

By Carmen Louise

"Look at the double chin, it wobbles when you talk."

I hear him as I sit in the passenger seat of the yellow range rover, or as we liked to call it, the Rangy. I look over at my dad, who's looking at me with such disgust. He looks back at the road and shakes his head. He continues to make inappropriate remarks about how I disgust him because of the cellulite on my legs, and the way I had my hair, etc. I sink into the seat and look out the window. Then I get slapped across the back of my head… "Are you listening?!" he grunts.

From the moment I can remember, I was programmed with the most negative and disturbing beliefs. I always had a roof over my head and food in front of me. So, I was cared for on the basic needs front. But behind closed doors, unspeakable things were happening, and guilt was imposed on me daily for having luxuries such as food.

I have childhood post-traumatic stress disorder, or CPTSD, resulting from severe childhood abuse. Yet I am proud and hold my head high on most days because I am a successful business woman. I have endured abuse from my father as early as I can remember. The very strategic psychological abuse has had lasting effects. He studied psychology and human behaviour in depth and used what he learned to 'program' me. He succeeded for most of my life.

I genuinely believed the worst about myself. Throughout my life, I had dark, intrusive thoughts. In addition to all the programming, I blamed myself for the physical and sexual abuse.

"I am fat and ugly. Hating myself [at the moment] is good motivation not to eat. Once I lose a lot of weight, then maybe I'll be happy. I need to somehow make my mum and dad proud of me. Dad will maybe love me."

This is part of one of the many letters I wrote to myself as a teenager. And to be honest, I left certain details out because they were pretty dark and involved how deserving I was of the self-harm I would inflict on myself. When I was ten, my mum would walk in on me and see scissors in my hand. She would panic and break down. I felt so pathetic as a human for most of my life. I believed what my father would tell me each day. My mum didn't know the extent of the abuse, and to protect her privacy, I won't go into the abuse she endured.

I had developed a habit of writing hate letters to myself. I would pledge to keep punishing myself. To vomit my food if I had to eat in front of others and inflicting self-harm. But I knew that if I committed suicide, I would break my mum's heart. Growing up, she was my best friend, and to this day, she doesn't realise how much she kept me alive. She told me daily that I was born to do great things, and that I had this bright light around me. She truly believed I was here to make a difference, and I stayed alive to make her proud and prove my dad wrong. So, from a young age, I knew I had to use my childhood to help others. It has become the silver lining to why I went through all that I did.

I committed my life to martial arts. I did this for many reasons, but the main one was to help women and children protect themselves from predators. I didn't realise that I would end up helping men too. In my early twenties, I worked in two gyms and then started to manage martial arts gyms. I was blessed to be able to attend sales and marketing training. For those who don't know, sales and marketing training go hand in hand with self-development training. It could be as simple as goal setting to reach sales targets or creating vision boards and identifying long-term life goals.

Eventually, I learned about affirmations, hypnosis, the Emotional Freedom Technique (EFT tapping), and Neuro-Linguistic Programming (NLP), which has been an ongoing process. However, I can tell you that each of these has changed my life. At some point, I went from only believing in scientific processes to believing in some of the most 'woo-woo' things out there. Now, I find myself somewhere in the middle.

As a woman in my thirties, I have the most clarity in my life ever, and I am very content with the existence I lead. This is not to say I won't be triggered or fall into past programming patterns. However, I am confident in the tools I have up my sleeve to live an extraordinary life. I am amazing and I am proud of who I am. I am the creator of my life, and I am not a victim.

Look at that! If I had known as a child that I would truly believe this one day, things would have been very different. But I went down the path I did, and I am so grateful because I am where I am today.

So how does someone like me, who was severely abused and believed herself to be the least worthy person on this earth - on such a deep seeded level - become someone who walks around and loves who she sees in the mirror?

I lived many years as a victim in my story and that sucked! I realised that existence was horrible. It took a while, but I transitioned from loathing myself, to now loving myself and trusting that I am here to help others love themselves, too, and no longer be a victim in their lives. I'm still human, and I continue to have my moments where I can't get my hair to sit right, or I put on mascara to add a little pep in my step, but I'm so aware of this being my journey. I take full responsibility for my mindset. And even when I'm feeling low, I still take responsibility for pulling myself out of it.

I quite recently took the biggest leap of faith in my whole life. Unfortunately, this led to so much uncertainty and so many triggering situations and moments where I felt so low. One challenging situation after another triggered the hell out of me! I started to drink more and felt myself turning into the victim. Yes, some shitty things happened to me, and I lost my way momentarily. But you know what… I found it again! I am human. It is my birth right. I was gifted the ability to feel from the moment

I was born. Emotions are not linear. I can't predict or control them. And when they build up, my world becomes chaotic. It happens to *every single person,* but not every single person takes control of their life.

When you feel so low and dark, I promise you the hardest thing in the world is to pull yourself out of it. I guarantee you; I've been there. No one can do it but you. You can have amazing support in your life, and while that may be helpful, *you are the one* that determines how you come out of those dark moments. If you are at the lowest of lows, you must find your reason 'why'. You have to find what works for you to get out of there. Mine is easy. From the moment I had my daughter, I knew that the best role model I could be for her was to lead by example. To love myself genuinely and to approach each day with love, gratitude and appreciation.

What is your why?

So here I come to my silver lining outlook that I apply every day.

Have you ever heard about the challenge where you don't complain for a certain number of days? Or the one where you wear a rubber band around your wrist and snap it every time you repeat an undesired behaviour you're trying to change? This is the silver lining challenge I had never heard of, and it has changed my life. I thought I had come up with it, but many are out there. You can google about silver lining challenges. I believe it's a wonderful challenge to share!

It's along the lines of consciously programming your mind to see, think and feel the positives first. It can be in day-to-day life or when you're dealing with people in your life that trigger you. But to stay with this theme, I'm going to share this process with the main focus being self-talk and belief.

First, I must add a wonderful acknowledgment to the subconscious mind. It is incredibly powerful! And it works for you in a multitude of ways. It's so hidden, yet it's always there! I highly recommend everyone to go down the path of upgrading their mind. I'm a huge advocate for always finding the best way for our bodies, minds, and emotions to function. I've always been baffled at people's care and attention to upgrading their cars, homes, and electronic devices. But they don't care much about the three main things they have with them 24/7. Instead, people fall into patterns of trashing their bodies, flooding their minds with trashy tv shows every day and masking their emotions through depressants such as alcohol. I'm not saying you can't do any of those things, but everything in moderation, hey!

So, what is a silver lining? It's that glowing line that traces around a grey cloud. I remember sitting in the car one day with my partner Jason, and we were racking our brains trying to figure out why it was called a silver lining. Admittedly, we thought of the clouds, but I was convinced that the colour around them was gold. Of course, we succumbed to doing a google search! The idea is that no matter how dark a situation may appear, you can always see the silver lining around it. It may be a small dark cloud with the sun behind it, glistening around the edges. And other times, the entire sky may be filled with grey clouds, but we always know the sun is just behind it. It may take a few minutes, a few hours, or even days, but the clouds will always part, and in some way, the sun will highlight the silver lining. Honestly, I still think the edges look gold at times, but realistically, the idea is all the same, whether it's a gold or silver lining.

A small actionable step to upgrading your way of thinking is to work on having a silver lining outlook. Choose a small number of days to commit – something like five to seven days. I recommend this so you can invest a lot of energy into committing to doing this without feeling overwhelmed. Once you've consciously committed to five to seven days a few times through, not only will it become a habit, but you will also be able to do it for longer periods of time. As a side note, if you can do it for longer, then hell yeah! Go for it!

Then commit! Commit to yourself, your friends, and your family, and get them onboard. Next, you need a diary. Preferably one you can write in, but you can also use an app on your phone. At the end of each day, write yourself a love letter about how proud of yourself and grateful you are. Add in situations throughout the day if you feel like it. Be honest! It's only for your eyes, and it's your one planned moment of the day to love and appreciate yourself. Here is an example:

Dear Carmen,

I am so proud of you! No matter what was thrown at me today, I saw the silver lining, took a deep breath, and continued on. Yes, it really sucks that my car costs $1,400 to get fixed, but I am so lucky the mechanic did a breakdown on all the costs so I could choose which options to choose. I'm so lucky to have a mum that was able to help me pay for the bill. And guess what! My car will be safe and roadworthy when I pick it up tomorrow! It's also funny because I had to teach BJJ tonight with a pink belt because my car unexpectedly stayed overnight, and my training gear was in there. It gave everyone a bit of a laugh.

(To add some context, this was a real situation. I had the option of feeling like a failure because I couldn't afford to get my car fixed and choosing to ruminate on the inconvenience of not having my car. I could have really fallen into the anger of feeling unprofessional teaching BJJ without my brown belt. However, I chose the silver linings outlook.)

Now I'm very aware that I cannot change what happened to me in my past and the programming that was inflicted on me. But my golly, it is my choice not to be a victim and to take control of the rest of my life. I know that trying to reprogram your mind can be a roller coaster. Some days are definitely harder than others. Some days the triggers catch you off guard and find you in situations where you want to escape, and that may not be a possibility. So, you either detach and disassociate, or have a full-blown outburst at someone, the situation or yourself. That's part of the healing journey.

Some may argue that seeing silver linings is pointless and that things happen because they happen, and they suck. But I argue back, "Well if it has happened and was always going to happen, whether you consider it being the universe, GOD or any other pre-planned situation, or you think there is only a physical existence with no spirituality or religion, wouldn't your experience be much nicer if you were to see a silver lining? Doesn't it take away some of the sting? Does it help make things feel more bearable? Doesn't it help you function just that little bit better throughout the day?"

I have yet to come across someone who disagrees.

Let's lead the way in seeing silver linings… share them with your loved ones, particularly your children.

ANA O'BRIEN

Ana lives in the city of Melbourne with her son's and daughter's family which includes two beautiful grandsons and two grand furry babies.

Ana was in security operations at the executive level for 22 years. Having to raise a family from a very early age, she found no time for university studies. Her experience came from working hard and adapting to her environment. A pioneer in her field of security solutions, Ana paved the way for the other women in her industry. She attributes her success to her ability to adapt, make decisions and to the reading of sci-fi novels.

Ana spends most of her time reading, playing with her grandchildren, cooking, travelling to wineries, visiting museums and zoos, sailing and catching her favourite movies. An admitted movie fanatic, she feeds her addiction to sci-fi by watching Netflix, Stan, Disney, and Stremio on Sunday afternoons. Ana is looking forward to writing more about sharing the light within you.

Chapter 7

Forgiveness Snapshot

By Ana O'Brien

I will start from the beginning. I was born in 1966 in a country that no longer exists. I am the daughter of a Hungarian mother and a father who was Serbian/Bulgarian/Croatian. I have a brother who was also born there, and a sister born two years after we immigrated to Australia. It wasn't just the four of us that immigrated to Australia; my youngest uncle was part of the family pack. My mother had raised her two youngest siblings since her mother's death when she was only 16 years old. My uncle would follow her throughout our lives.

When I first began writing, my life played like a motion picture in my head: significant moments, life-changing and life-commencing moments. The beauty of being a woman is that we are all born with the gift of life and intuition.

From a very early age, I knew there was not just a physical but spiritual connection to the earth. In my dreams, I flew, and on the earth plain (physical), I always felt the same. The joy a new day brought me. I was here, and I made it. Let me explain. In all my lifetimes, it has always been about fighting to live and survive and protecting the weak. Some of them had always been with me and followed me throughout the ages.

Imagine meeting somebody, knowing them instantly without having met them before. I met a woman last year, and the instant we looked at each other, we both said, "I know you!" We talked for over two hours, going through the people, places, and family. We did not have a physical connection. I explained that I had known her as a brunette. Her expression was one of surprise. She told me she had always been a blonde but immediately insisted I come to her home to see something. When we go there, she took me by the hand and walked me towards the lounge room. She turned slightly to the right and then raised her arm to show me a picture of herself as a brunette surrounded by cats. Her youngest daughter drew her that way and told her at the time, that was how she saw her mother. We recognised each other as familiars. I instantly loved her and she loved me. Soul sisters.

I have always felt the need to protect others, stand-up for the weak and fight for those who couldn't fight for themselves. So the search for justice ramped up and stayed with me.

It started early for me.

The first moment in time was around my eighth birthday. My mother had to go into surgery and would require time to heal after the operation. In those days, we were part of the first wave of immigrants from my country and had no women in the family to help look after children. So my mother decided she would send my sister back to a monastery run by nuns and priests. This place was not safe; it was not good and brought horrors to both of us.

I was ill with kidney disease then, and my mother could not send me back with my sister. At the time, I couldn't express myself. So, I'd cling to my mother's legs and beg her not to send my sister back to that place. She could not console me. I remember her asking me, "Do you really think I want to send her there? I have no choice. She needs care while I am in the hospital, and the men can't take care of her." So off she went. What happened to us as children forever changed our innocence and what we knew of the world. We had learned of cruel, disgusting, and sinister things adults could do. I vowed to make sure nobody ever hurt my sister again.

Anyone caught bullying, picking on, insulting, or looking at her differently would get what was coming to them. Whether it was verbal or physical, it just happened. This included my uncles, aunts, brother, boyfriends and partners. The list was endless, and I was without mercy. My sister was sweet, gentle, and creative and came back differently. The dynamic between my mother and myself had altered too. I did not see my mother as my sister's protector, and I did not know that she had no choice. My sister returned with demons; they followed and awakened in the house. That is truly another story. When trauma enters a young life, it also opens other doorways.

I had always had a feeling, the gut, the intuition or whatever you want to call it, the knowing. I just knew I felt the answer. I do not know how to explain it, except it felt right. I have said things to people without preempting it. The words come out without me thinking about them. People would say, "How did you know that this would happen?" and, "You told me we were going to win." or "How did you know?" The incidents I refer to in my story propelled me to who I am today.

I was nine years old when the next incident occurred and thrust me into the person I have become. It was 1975, and I was in the children's ward of the Queen Victorian Hospital. I had a kidney disease that one in one million survived, and at the time, it had taken my life more than once. I died on the table a few times and got revived. This particular night I was lying awake. I remember coming in and out of sleep. At one stage, a doctor and nurse stood at the foot of my bed. They whispered, "She won't make it until the morning." They were talking about me, and I remember crying, and I could not get consoled. I don't know who called my parents, but I remember that I felt my mum's hand in mine, the brush of her fingers through my hair, and my eyes gazing into her stormy blue-grey eyes. "Tell me why you are crying, little cat," she asked with a mixture of Hungarian/Yugoslavian in her voice. I told her I had heard I would not make it 'til the morning. I got to know the look on her face as I grew older; it was the who-dared-say-that-to-you look. But what she said was the most profound statement.

"What have I told you, baby? Who can tell you if you're going to live or die?"

My reply was, "GOD," and my mother looked at me and said, "Do you see GOD here?"

I said, "NO!"

"Good! Well, then…" she quietly whispered, "I know you are tired, baby. I will understand if you want to close your eyes. Mummy will always love you, but if you don't want to close your eyes, then fight, baby!"

Yes, I lived beyond their expectations. Do you know I lost count of how many times I would not make it? I didn't expect to live beyond my teens, much less my twenties.

Unfortunately, I would never be able to conceive a child. Men who were doctors said this and told my family to prepare for the worst. Doctors told me repeatedly that I was going to die. The male doctors had an "I am GOD attitude." No compassion, empathy or understanding. Yes, I did die. Did I see a light? No.

At fourteen, I did something that astonished the medical practitioners and my parents. I stopped taking my thirty-six steroid tablets and threw them down the sink. My body told me to stop taking them and that they would inevitably kill me, not the disease. I heeded the warning and stopped taking them. Then I embarked on a vegetarian diet which included fish and sometimes poultry. My family cooked pork, lamb, and beef with everything. I took up the diet and did not drink tea or coffee, just water and hot chocolate. I listened to my body over the years. I was hospitalised for over six months and refused to take the tablets. Finally, I told my mum I had to stop and would rather die than take them another day. My body, my skin, and my health all changed for the better. I lived beyond my teens.

I never thought I would fall in love, but I did. I was eighteen, and the man I had fallen in love with was seven years older. I knew from the time I met him that he was mine. When he decided he wanted me in his life, I had to disclose that I would never be able to conceive and that I would understand if he did not want to be with me. He looked at me at the time and said there are other ways we can get a child; plenty of kids need love. I was not an incubator.

This was a magical moment. I knew he loved me, and it was okay that I couldn't conceive. When I took him home to meet my parents, my mother told him I would never be able to have children. It appalled him that she did not even think to consult me. Yep, I lost it. She thought I wouldn't tell the person I was sharing my life with about my inability to provide children or the possibility of not surviving through my mid-twenties. I am not surprised because she had ideas about who she felt I was. Not the person I had become who held exceptionally high value.

During the years I was in the hospital, I was assaulted and raped by three doctors. My mother once asked me, "What could I have done?" I did not speak English and the head nurse, along with the interpreter (the cleaner), told her what had happened to me. Then she asked, "What action would you like us to take?" My mother did nothing; they did nothing.

The funny thing is, I got pregnant! My father was so happy he didn't tell people I was engaged… he told everyone he would be a grandpa!

For the record, my mother never acknowledged what my sister and I endured for years at the hands of the priests so long ago. The trauma was too much for my sister. She was never the same, so I became overprotective and spoiled her. The fact was all the incidents became one incident for both of us. I forgave my mother, and I forgave them, but not their actions. I made myself strong by understanding that it was only the body they took. Not the soul attached; this they would never own in any way. The reality was that my mother could not accept the trauma she went through, so how was she going to accept what had happened to me.

Very few people in my life knew what happened to me… even my ex-husband. My sister told my ex-partner, and even my children didn't know until ten years ago. Do I suffer? Yes, with post-traumatic stress disorder (PTSD). I can't handle people standing over me or being told I can't do something. I have learned how to build walls, and to trust in myself.

There is one more piece that I believe is quintessential to why I am the way I am. Faith, belief and trust in myself made me strong. It was another test, another challenge in who I was and what I believed. The universe will only give us what she knows we can handle. So here it is …

Many people have spoken of their grief over the loss of a child. Everyone has an opinion, some believe that we choose our parents, so our children have chosen us. However, I am of the understanding that it was their journey too, no matter how short.

My daughter was only ten months old when I found out I was four months pregnant, which was strange. I still had my cycles. I was very skinny and fit, riding bikes and swimming so there was no indication I was pregnant. I discovered the pregnancy after finishing my course on first aid with St. John Ambulance. One autumn Thursday night, I drove home through Melbourne's Kings Street. Suddenly everything went dark, and I was blind behind the wheel in the farthest lane. Luckily, I had slowed down and felt for the hazard lights. I hoped somebody saw something. The angels were watching over me.

My ex-husband's friend owned the hotdog stand across the road from one of the biggest night spots. He came to the rescue, managed to contact my ex-husband for help and it came. I had refused to go to the hospital, saying it was probably an unusual migraine. But I did go to the emergency room the next day. They checked the usual vitals and did some bloodwork. When the results came back, the doctor announced that I was pregnant. I told him he was FUCKED! Do I look pregnant? I don't even feel pregnant. He concurred and asked if he could do an internal. Yep, absolutely! He had washed his hands, made his preps, had a feel and then turned around to say he was getting a second opinion. The head of obstetrics joined us. The look of concern was that I was over four months pregnant. It felt wrong in every way. I met my husband at our friend's restaurant. My husband was surprised and overwhelmed and said, "We will get through it." I just told him it did not feel right. "It will be alright, dear. We'll go get it checked out by our obstetrician."

I knew from the beginning that Josh's time was limited, and he was not coming home with me. Apparently, my son Joshua only wanted to experience the birth. The most difficult part of this journey was my family and friends trying to work through their grief for me. My father blamed himself for what happened to me and felt that GOD was punishing me for the transgressions of his youth. My mother thought she was going to lose her child again and lost a grandchild instead. She grieved for my son. My sister and brother were just grateful that I survived again and now understood why I did not want to prepare for this baby. The saddest of this was that my husband was not there to support me. Yes, he was at my bedside, but he was not there. His family leaned on him for support, so when it was time for us to grieve together, his response was, "Not you too."

I carried the baby for seven and a half months. Throughout the pregnancy, the baby was making me ill. Nobody believed me, including my husband. I was alone, except for my baby girl. From that one comment, my marriage and trust were never the same. However, I am grateful to have been blessed with a third child, my son, Benjamin. I am honoured that he chose me to be his mother. My children have brought so much joy to my life, and I relived moments through them. And our Josh watches over us as our guardian angel.

This is the first time I have written about myself. I have never felt so vulnerable nor so exhilarated. My life is constantly evolving, so my story continues. I survived a disease that has killed many others, and they told me I couldn't have children. As a result, I didn't want to engage in relationships because I didn't want people I love to suffer with me. Then, I met a man who accepted me as I was. With him I had three children. In all this, I had never spoken to him or anyone about what had happened to me. Not to protect me but to protect them. It did not break me, it did not own me, and it never will. Despite what has happened, my journey has truly been wondrous.

I have learned to adapt in life, which has put me in good stead. I have worked in male-dominated industries all my life. I had always taken risks stepping out of my comfort zones regarding security solutions. New technologies enabled me to provide fully integrated solutions that met and exceeded clients' expectations. Most of my counterparts stuck with what was safe. I stretched and challenged the norm. I do the same thing in life. I have been told, repeatedly, that I had bigger balls than most men! I am fearless, and I'm not scared to take risks. Life without risk and adventure is just an existence. I have learned to be present, live like it is my last day, love without condition, laugh until my insides hurt, and always dream.

This is me.

Kate Southall

After many years of sacrificing the life she deserved, Kate Southall made a choice to create financial freedom for herself and to live life on her terms with purpose.

Kate was a successful owner of an educational institute for more than fifteen years. With qualifications in psychology, business, and marketing she inspired over 10,000 students and 200 employees Australia wide.

In her mid-forties, Kate moved out of the corporate world and into a world of health and wellness, inspiring others to seek their true calling. All of Kate's programs support women to ignite the warrior within, thrive in business and life, love everything they do, and Live Life with Purpose.

Email Kate to claim your gift of a 30-minute Clarity Call.

Email: kate@freedomempowermentimpact.com.au

Facebook: https://www.facebook.com/KateSouthall2020

Website: https://www.freedomempowermentimpact.com.au/

CHAPTER 8

Becoming a Courageous Woman

by Kate Southall

By the age of seven, I had survived a loveless childhood. I learned to be invisible to stay safe. Unfortunately, my parents were incapable of caring for children. They were either stoned, high on pills or mentally vacant. We all have heard the saying, "humans need a licence to drive, but not to have a child." I often think of this saying and wonder why my parents couldn't see the gift they had been given that some others never receive. It's funny, I actually can't recollect a time of feeling connected to my parents. There are brief flashes of laughter, feelings of comfort, and moments of fun, but mostly there is just a deep feeling of loss. A loss of childhood, a loss of love never received, a loss of opportunity to start my life the right way – in a loving and supported way.

We moved many times. I attended eleven primary schools, many of which I don't remember. I learned from a very young age not to connect so as not to feel the pain of moving on. It was a lonely childhood. The time I spent with my parents was always in a partially built house that was being renovated. Sometimes we'd share a room with another sibling. Other times we'd have to sleep in the hallway; it depended on how much renovation was going on.

Sometimes we had money, but more often, we did not.

Our imprinting years are between zero and seven years old.

At the age of seven, my mother decided to take me and my older sister, who was twelve, into a "community lifestyle" shared among families. Some may refer to this as a Cult.

What I endured during this rather short period of time in my life has created a lifetime of pain, trauma, and the constant need for me to find courage.

Courage not to become a victim of abuse but to be a survivor. Courage not to hate but to look for the beauty in life. Courage to believe that there would be more for me in this life and that what I had experienced in the first seven years was not my complete story.

It is amazing to imagine what a young girl, just seven years old, may experience, and how she creates a lifelong belief system that could affect almost every decision she makes.

I am far from healed from the first seven years of my life. However, I wake up every day prepared to take on anything that the Universe wants me to receive because I know that I will bloody take it on, learn from it and keep walking forward towards the life I know I want … the life that I know I deserve.

By the age of fourteen, I had escaped the community lifestyle. Well, it isn't quite that simple. However, this is a chapter, not a novel!

So, I escaped the community lifestyle to be handed to a Catholic Church to be looked after by nuns. I was there for a short time before a man, who they called my father, but I had never actually met, arrived to take me to his home... or so I thought. The car drive from Sydney to Melbourne was a nine hour drive I will never forget. I remember looking at the back of this tall man's head as he sat in the driver seat of his old Valiant car. The music seemed dark; the air seemed heavy, and the mood seemed tense. I sat in the passenger seat behind him, not speaking a word as it didn't appear that my voice wanted to be heard. I remember him as an angry man, distant and unreachable. Even though I felt quite terrified at the time, I always felt that I was looking at myself in the mirror.

It was a brief encounter, this so-called father-daughter experience, because he basically dropped me off at an unknown location to fend for myself.

Surviving up to this point of my young life took sheer determination. Not having a secure, safe home, or one I felt wanted in, meant I moved around in foster homes until I could change things for myself. And that is what I did.

I spent most of my teenage years in as many "family" homes as possible. It was important for me to experience the complexities and connections of different family units. I needed to get a sense of what it might have felt like to be loved by my parents. I knew that it would be important for me to see, through my own eyes, how that connection and the unconditional relationship between parent and child shapes a child's sense of self and worth in their world.

I worked seven days a week, finishing school and running to the local General Store, which was 1.5 kilometres away. I would get there in fifteen minutes, just in time to start my shift at 3:30 pm. I worked until we closed at 11:00 pm. I worked every weekend and every public holiday, including Christmas. I did this knowing that if I did, I would be able to purchase my first car and first home at eighteen, and that's exactly what I did.

By the age of twenty-one, this young girl was a woman and I got married. It was short-lived, lasting just six months. I often think about this choice in my life. I can see now why I married so early and why I had four bridesmaids, a big white dress with all the bells and whistles. Why did I invite as many people as possible to attend the wedding even though I barely knew them? I wanted to appear to others like I had it all. That my life was perfect. The house, the nice car, the good job, the husband. I did have those things, even a husband that truly loved me. But how can you be loved, and love another, when you still carry so much pain? I walked away from the experience, ready for the next chapter of my life. I believed my short-lived marriage was just another part of my life story.

By the age of twenty-nine, I was an accomplished woman in many ways. I had two degrees and had started my first business seeking the life of an entrepreneur. I drove a beautiful convertible Astra, was ready to start a property portfolio, and felt like I could take on anything. I didn't realise, though, that the 'things' I had purchased, and the life I was living now, didn't mean that I was being true to myself. I was in so much emotional pain and was using alcohol and work to push the pain down. So, the Universe decided to give me another life lesson.

I lost a kidney from a family kidney disease, inherited by a father I never really knew or understood. It stopped me in my tracks for a bit, but I was not yet at a stage in my life where I could recognise the signs. I truly believe that the Universe gives us signs along the way – sliding door moments. I was blind to many of these signs for most of my life. I would never allow myself the opportunity to receive. Although I was courageous, I was still just a girl that felt pain, loss and fear.

By thirty-six, I had four degrees and owned a successful seven-figure business. In addition, I had a beautiful home near the ocean, the car I had always dreamed of having, a mini convertible, and a property portfolio. It was funny, though. The more I surrounded myself with 'things', the more I created a life of 'wealth', the more I began to feel hollow and alone. During this time of my life, I was diagnosed with Type 1 Diabetes and lived in an abusive, unhappy relationship.

It was hard to imagine why I would experience more challenges when I had survived so much already. I was not yet able to understand why people receive these types of lessons to learn. Why did I need to work so fucking hard to live? Why had I found myself in an emotionally abusive relationship when I had already endured abuse on so many levels?

I dug deep at this stage of my life. I did what I only knew how and what to do in moments like this – I worked harder, achieved more, and ignored the abuse. I found it incredibly difficult to accept that I would now have to live with and manage a chronic illness for the rest of my life.

During the first few years of this diagnosis, I punished myself many times. I couldn't accept that my independence, spontaneity, and unstoppable way now needed to be 'managed'. I had many hospital trips caused only by my choice to push the limits. Finally, I decided to embrace the woman I knew I was -- a courageous woman. I took back my life and lived.

By forty-three, I had lost my seven-figure business, home, car, and properties and finally left my abusive partner. With my four-year-old son, I returned to my place of healing, The Dandenong Ranges, and even though I had nothing, I honestly had just enough.

An interesting reflection here… It may seem as if I had it all, but really, I had superficially set up an existence that didn't belong to me. I was successful, and yes, I deserved this. However, I still felt dislike for myself. I didn't believe that I deserved this level of success and to be living the lifestyle that I was living. I still had not confronted my past. I needed to feel the pain. I needed to truly believe that my young life was not what I deserved. I needed to find the positive learnings from these experiences and turn them into my superpowers. I needed to believe in myself. I needed to see my worth. I needed to love myself and allow myself to feel love.

So, it is here that I stopped just long enough to realise that I have been surviving, not living. So, I began to reflect on a life that may not be considered a chosen one for some, but for me, it was the life I had been given.

I set up a hiking & fitness business and took on a double degree in Naturopathy and Nutritional Medicine. I qualified in Hike Leading and Fitness Instructing, lived with very little and earned just enough to pay the bills. But do you know what I did have? I had plenty of time to reflect on my life and begin the healing process.

This year, I turn fifty.

So, let's recap the past seven years.

I have spent the past seven years working on myself. I have come to terms with some (not all) of the injustices I experienced during my life, particularly in my younger years. I am learning to feel more, love more, and need more. I believe that I was a good girl, that what happened to me wasn't my fault, and that I am a good woman. I allow myself to feel the pain from my past and the present. I welcome the things that trigger me and lean into them, for I know I will learn and grow from them.

I have two successful businesses – a coaching business and a hiking business. I have six degrees and am an established and highly sought-after life and business coach. I love what I do. I love that I help other women ignite the warrior within to thrive and want more. I support as many people as possible to bring adventure into their lives and walk this beautiful place we call Earth.

I truly believe that anything is possible if you believe in yourself and know your worth. I live my life making sure that everything I do is with intentional purpose.

In 2020, when Covid hit, I had seven surgeries in eight months. Was it tough? Yes. Did I understand why? Yes. But you see, the work I had done on myself, and continue to do, has given me enough awareness of the signs. My body showed me the pain and fear that I still needed to work on, and they presented themselves when I couldn't to distract myself with a busy lifestyle.

In 2021, I achieved a challenge in my Coaching Group to earn $100,000 in one hundred days. I made $101,000 in seventy-two days and received three awards - 6-Figure Club, P100, and Consistent $10k Months.

In 2022, I will be a co-author in two books (this being one of them!), and I am writing my first book that is being published at the end of the year. Becoming a full-time writer and public speaker is a lifelong dream of mine.

I am present for my beautiful and kind son. I am learning how to let him see me and feel my immense love for him as his mother but sometimes find it hard to show. It can be hard to show your child the love they need and deserve when you never had it.

My life is full of awesomeness, and I seek this willingly and enthusiastically. Women were created and put in this world to be awesome. I have tattoos on my body, and they are sayings that I live by: Live in The Moment, and More Zena Than Princess. I also have Dragonflies that symbolise change, transformation, adaptability, and self-realisation. And I have an Infinity Symbol in honour of my son, which signifies the concept of limitlessness eternity.

I tell my story to inspire other women to believe that they, too, have the courage they need to seek more in life, live life on their terms, and *live with purpose, not just to survive!*

Yes, there are many things in my life that, if I had to choose whether to experience them, I would have said, "Fuck NO!" I deserved so much better. I may not have had these choices then, but the lesson I would love to pass on is that the moment you can make the choices you want in your life, then make them.

Find the courage and live life on your terms.

Find what lights you up.

Find a way to ask for more of yourself, and just go for it!

Don't allow the treatment from others, or events that are out of your control, define who you are.

Don't allow this life, your life, to go by and not ever ask yourself, *"What do I truly desire?"*

Dare to be Great! xxx

GRACE WEE

An optometrist by trade, Grace Wee travelled Australia servicing regional and country towns. Within a very short amount of time, Grace's father passed away suddenly, she experienced a break-up, and was in a major car accident that caused her to re-evaluate her relationship with time and money.

Grace grew her own personal financial portfolio to over $40K in under two years and felt compelled to empower other women to do the same. She opened Grace Wee Coaching and teaches women to honour their time and self-worth by growing their wealth and confidence with her signature programs and coaching.

Being a certified NLP Practitioner and competitive black belt in Tae Kwon Do helps Grace to live her best life. In her spare time, she is the Treasurer for Eyes4Everest, an organisation that serves Nepalese in the Solukhumbu region with access to eye tests. As part of organising these volunteer missions, Grace trekked to Everest Basecamp in 2016.

Chapter 9

The Most Precious Commodity

By Grace Wee

My phone vibrates, and the screen lights up. Dad is calling.

My Dad, who lives in Malaysia, normally rings me now and again to say a quick hello. But, I was attending an optometry conference. So, I could not pick up when he called.

Later, when I stepped out of the conference room, I called him back. He usually answers with his big, booming, cheery voice, "Good morning, my beautiful daughter." Except for this time, it wasn't Dad.

"Grace, there's been a car accident, and your dad is in a critical condition…"

It was Meng who worked for Dad. She sounded hysterical. Through her sobs, she told me that Dad had been in a car accident. He was now in the hospital in a remote town in Malaysia and was in critical condition. I felt that I shouldn't overreact first without knowing the full details of the situation.

Later I discovered that the car that Dad was in overturned. Dad suffered injuries, went unconscious, and was in the hospital, where they were trying to revive him.

My heart dropped like a tonne of bricks. Being in Sydney, there was nothing much I could do except pray.

Minutes later, Dad passed away.

He was suddenly gone. I didn't even have a chance to say goodbye. It all happened so quickly.

At first, I couldn't move. Then came the tears and I started crying uncontrollably.

Later that day, I was going to give a talk with the other committee members of a charity organisation, Eyes4Everest. After telling them the news, I went straight home to prepare for the next flight out. Little did I know that my life would dramatically change after this.

I have lived a relatively normal life compared to others. I came to Australia when I was very young. Like most Asian kids, I was taught that it was vitally important to get good grades, do well in school and university so that you can get a good, respectable professional job that pays well.

Like any Asian kid, that's what I did.

I came in the top three for Year Six, went on to a selective high school, finished with a score in the high 90s, and went on to complete an optometry degree. After graduating, I landed a secure nine to five optometry job that paid well. Furthermore, I went on and completed my master's in optometry, which made my parents proud.

While growing up in Sydney, my father stayed in Malaysia to run his architecture company. He was the breadwinner while my mum raised my siblings and me in Sydney. Financially, we had a stable upbringing. My mum saved most of the money my dad gave her. And she never lived above her means. As a result, we never saw any financial hardship, although we did not have a lot of things. If there was financial hardship, they hid it well. What I had was good home-cooked food, a comfortable home and the ability to participate in extracurricular activities such as piano and dancing, as well as go on holidays.

Despite my financial stability during childhood and doing well in school, what was happening deep down was my struggle with self-confidence and self-worth. Being the youngest, I believed those older than me were smarter and knew more than me.

I was fairly introverted, and to gain love and acceptance from my parents, teachers and friends, I became good at conforming to what was expected of me. I relied on the validation of others, whether I was doing well or not, to the point it was at the expense of my happiness.

If you were good at something, under an Asian upbringing, you were told not to boast about it. Instead, it was encouraged to downplay your strengths because humility is a good virtue.

As I became proficient at conforming, I would be a team player, following and doing my part. However, I did not have the courage to step up to be a leader due to my lack of confidence.

On the other hand, my dad was always full of confidence. He was an action taker and would always do what he said he'd do. If naysayers told him it was impossible, he made it possible.

Because of this, family, friends, and business associates often came to him for guidance and held a lot of respect for Dad.

As my father, he was my safety net. Even though he was ridiculously busy with work, he guided me through any challenges or problems I had. It didn't matter how insignificant or small they seemed. His confidence, encouragement, and faith in me helped me build my confidence and overcome my insecurities.

Suddenly, my safety net was no longer there.

As I was grieving, I became regretful. My biggest regret was being angry at him for not looking after himself better. I regretted not spending enough quality time with him. I wished I could turn back time and make things right.

Adding to the grief, my partner and I also broke up the same year. I found out he was seeing someone else. Being a big part of my life for eight years, suddenly, he became a person I hardly knew. The trust was gone. I came out feeling more broken.

Shortly after my break-up, I found myself in a car accident. I lost control of the car, swerved, and did a nose-dive off the motorway in a regional town three hours from Sydney. Fortunately, I didn't have any injuries. However, I could not say the same for my car. The front of it was completely smashed and was a complete write-off.

Since the accident, I did not have the emotional capacity to travel for a few months. However, there were still lots of things that needed to be done in Malaysia after Dad had passed. Unfortunately, with the amount of travelling back and forth from

Australia to Malaysia, going back to full-time employment was not an option. These also presented new challenges.

With the amount of travelling I was doing, and without a job, expenses were mounting substantially. So I began to locum, providing temporary relief to practices all over Australia who needed an optometrist. It was something I never planned to do; however, it provided a solution where I could get income and still travel between Sydney and Malaysia when I needed to.

As a result of losing my dad, the break-up and the accident, my life suddenly changed in a heartbeat. I went from having a secure job, being in a steady relationship, practising Taekwon-Do and going out with friends on weekends to being a grieving, self-employed locum with no income security, single and constantly travelling.

I struggled with my confidence to navigate through life's sudden challenges. I wasn't confident enough to weather this on my own. With my dad as my safety net gone, I felt I had no one to turn to for guidance. I also struggled with trust and finding my self-worth after my break-up. The car accident escalated those feelings substantially. I struggled to cope emotionally.

I would think to myself...

Why do these things keep happening to me?

Why is my life so shitty?

Why was Dad gone so soon?

Why can't I have the life I used to have?

Why did he cheat on me?

I didn't ask for this.

It's not fair!

I would have sudden bursts of frustration and sadness, breaking down and crying uncontrollably. One night, I did just that and burst into tears. I had never felt so lonely and helpless in my life.

That same night, I decided that I didn't want this anymore. I wanted my life to change.

Albert Einstein once said, "We cannot solve the same problems with the same thinking we used when we created them."

I began exploring how thinking differently would empower me to navigate through this mess. Gradually, I practised replacing my current thoughts with new, empowering, constructive ones.

How can I move forward with my life?

What has my life blessed me with?

What am I grateful for?

What lessons can I learn so I can make my life better?

How can I improve?

What does living my best life look like?

How can I move towards it?

I realised that it was up to me to choose to shift my thoughts and not let my negative thoughts control me. It was a game changer. Later I discovered that all of these events had a common theme.

It was time… specifically, my appreciation for time.

With Dad gone, I began to whole-heartedly appreciate that life is precious and time is valuable. The break-up helped me appreciate the value of my time and the importance of with whom I spend it. The car accident gave me with a second chance in life and taught me to appreciate how I spend my time.

So, I made a promise to myself to live my best life. We are all given 24 hours a day. However, once passed, we can never get that time back. Money, on the other hand, when lost, can always be made.

I spent time on myself. I gave myself the self-care and love I deserved and invested in improving myself, which led me to discover the world of personal development and life coaching. As part of my personal development journey, I began training for the Taekwon-Do World Championships.

The secrets I discovered to creating change in your life starts with being committed, consistent and disciplined. It may even challenge you to become resourceful when times are hard, when things do not go to plan or when situations are not ideal.

Working towards competing in the World Championships, I had to get resourceful about training with the frequent travelling I was doing. Travelling back and forth between Australia and Malaysia for work meant I could not consistently train in the dojang (training centre). My life on-the-go meant that my training had to be on-the-go, too. So, I trained in hotel rooms, parks, and different training centres to meet my commitments.

I learned that your thoughts and attitudes about your commitments and goals impact your results and everything you do, even when the odds are against you.

When training for the World Championships, the odds were against me. These odds included having no world-level tournament experience. I was in my mid-30's and considered "old" for my level. Apart from competing with others who were younger, stronger and more flexible than me, I only had one chance to compete in World Championships due to age eligibility.

The 'disempowered' version of me would have focused solely on the lack of experience and age and decided it would have been better to quit. However, the 'empowered' version chose to become stronger, despite my age and lack of experience.

One of my coaches imparted this powerful quote, which still resonates with me today.

"The reason why you won't can also be the reason why you will."

How you choose to think, and feel is entirely up to you. My decision to adopt the 'empowered' version of myself led to my unwavering commitment to my training. As a result, I had the opportunity to represent Australia in the 2019 Taekwon-Do World Championships. During this journey, I participated in many competitions and tournaments for experience, one of which was a different Taekwon-Do World Tournament, and I won gold.

Not bad for someone who had odds against her!

Had I chosen to adopt the 'disempowered' version of myself, none of this would have happened.

The most valuable takeaway from my journey was learning that I can overcome any challenges thrown at me. I proved to myself that I am worthy enough for bigger and better things.

You may be reading this and may be going through similar challenges. Perhaps your challenges are more significant than mine. But, no matter the odds against you, I am confident you can overcome and break through them.

Part of my commitment to living my best life was to ensure my own financial well-being. So, a stable financial foundation became my focus. Fortunately, my dad made sure my mum would be financially okay. But how many women are fortunate enough to be in this position? With the stories I hear, not a lot of them. And I didn't want to be one of them.

Time is infinitely more valuable than money. Yet, most people spend a significant portion of their lives trading time for money, probably in jobs they are not truly passionate about. Is that the best way to live your life?

I had a new challenge this time. How do you start growing wealth sustainably without trading your time? How do you start with zero knowledge and experience?

Instead of trading my time for money, I discovered how to leverage my time to grow my money. Thus, my journey led to the realm of investing. While saving is a good habit, it is also risky to keep all the money in the bank with the dollar devaluing each day. The stock market, by far, is the easiest entry point to making your money grow.

Even with a small investment, you can experience the true power of compounding, making your money grow while sleeping, thus leveraging your time. It happens in the background while you get on with your day-to-day activities. For me, what started out as a $500 investment, grew to a $40K portfolio within two years. The total contribution was under $20K, and the money grew by $20K with a portfolio of stocks and cryptocurrency.

And my portfolio is still growing, still compounding.

I became passionate about investing, and I became committed to empowering more women to take control and make their money grow.

If you are looking into investing, starting from scratch, and have no idea where to start, start investing in yourself first.

If you value time and want to get results quicker, you must invest in a coach who is successful at what they do. A brilliant coach knows what works and what doesn't and helps identify your blind spots, which saves you valuable time and gives you faster results.

When it came to growing my money, I invested in a money and investment coach, which led me to have a $40K portfolio in 2 years. Alternatively, it may have taken much longer to get there had I chosen to figure it out myself.

In Taekwon-Do, I was fortunate enough to have two grandmasters coaching me for the World Championships. They helped me discover the importance of staying consistent and committed to my training. They held me accountable, and I discovered how to be resourceful when times were hard.

I invested in a life coach who introduced me to the importance of a great mindset. So, instead of focusing on things that are disempowering, I focus on things that are empowering. Most importantly, if you want to get good at something, take action, implement it, and make it happen. These principles apply to any area in your life; this is how I did it when I went on my wealth creation journey.

Last but not least, I wish to share one more thing.

Celebrate your wins, even your small ones. Success and confidence are built on a series of small victories. Do not forget to celebrate them. Don't waste your energy and time focusing on disempowering thoughts that put you down.

You are more than what you give yourself credit for. You are worthy, and your time is precious. Who you spend time with and how you spend your time is important. Surround yourself with people who lift you up… even if it means investing in them.

Ultimately, live your best life, whatever that may be for you!

Conclusion

So, there you have it!

When you find the way to your dreams, you can never go back, and the compulsion to share the journey for the benefit of all becomes irresistible.

This book contains collection of stories and anecdotes from amazing women who dare to believe that there is more, that they deserve more and have taken the leap in exploring their universal potential. Each author now lives a much larger, fulfilling life in a constant state of wonder. I feel privileged to be counted among these courageous women who contributed to this book.

It is not an easy thing to expose their vulnerabilities so that you can learn from their experiences. They reveal stories that they have kept to themselves for so long. These authors open themselves to you and shine a light on their pain and regrets. In doing so, they hope that they may find healing, closure, and resolve. But most of all, they desire to inspire you, dear reader.

They want you to know that we all go through tough times. But good or bad, it's not the challenge that matters. It's the lessons we learn along the way.

I hope you found a little bit of yourself in these stories, and you realise that you, too, can make the paradigm shift from simply surviving to wondrously thriving. There's nothing to fear. You can change. You've got this!

If you enjoyed this book, we'd appreciate it if you'd hop on over to Amazon and write a review. This way, the authors will know they did – indeed - have an impact! Thank you in advance for sharing this journey with us.

Remember, at the end of the day, live your life all-in and full-out.

Most Importantly, be committed to *Living True to You!*

With love,

Catherine Chan-Kwa

www.ingramcontent.com/pod-product-compliance
Lightning Source LLC
Chambersburg PA
CBHW071715040426
42446CB00011B/2079